A Treasury
of
Beautiful Dolls

Doll-makers, an illustration from *The Graphic Christmas Number, 1878*
(Author's Collection)

A Treasury
of
Beautiful Dolls

by John Noble

with color plates by Peter Reinstorff
Foreword by Dorothy, Elizabeth, and Evelyn Coleman

WEATHERVANE BOOKS
New York

For Father Robert Clement

Foreword

One usually associates dolls with girls. The fact that some boys express more than a passing interest in dolls may come as an unexpected revelation to many people. As a schoolboy the author of this volume was so fascinated by a Victorian toy owned by one of his fellows that he traded a new plaything for this intriguing antique object. Unlike most toys that a child owns and plays with, the interest in this one did not wane. Still in the possession of the author, the ceramic cigar-shaped whistle with a child's figure astride it marked the beginning of a lifelong absorption in the times and objects of the nineteenth century. This interest has centered on playthings, especially dolls.

John Noble, a native of London, was born within the sound of Bow Bells. His education included some years in art school. He, in his turn, has taught and is a practicing artist. This training has given him unique qualifications for the task of viewing objects and communicating ideas about them. While pursuing his professions, John Noble was searching out and collecting antiques as well as lecturing and writing about his finds. By an unusual coincidence, of which the author was unaware at the time, he resided for several years at 3 Rathbone Place, formerly the home of Mme. Augusta Montenari, a famous manufacturer of wax dolls.

In 1960 Mr. Noble came to visit America and has lived here ever since. After a short time he found employment at the Museum of the City of New York, where he became curator of their noted Toy Collection. This is the only curatorial position devoted exclusively to toys in a major American museum.

Today dolls and toys usually form a part of the decorative-arts collections in museums. Until very recently the museums often unjustly stored away and forgot the dolls; they have also been assigned to the costume collections, where the outfits have been studied but the dolls themselves ignored. Thanks to the efforts of scholarly and sensitive people like John Noble, old dolls are beginning to be recognized as important historical artifacts; they reflect both the artistic modes and the social norms of the day. *A Treasury of Beautiful Dolls* greatly enhances our appreciation of dolls by allowing us to study them according to the ideals and fashions which they reflect. Throughout the book the dolls have been skillfully selected, and the author has endeavored to present only dolls that are in clothes contemporary with their manufacture.

Clothes on dolls can tell us more about the dolls—and the clothes—than we might ordinarily know and will also frequently help in confirming or modifying the recorded histories of the dolls. For example, the bride and groom shown on page 123 came to the author's collection with a note relating their early history. Written by a descendant of the original owner, the history read as follows: "The girl who owned these dolls was born in 1850 and lived in Oakland, a small town in Maine. The young miss received this pair of dolls for her twelfth birthday in 1862, and they had been especially dressed as if for their wedding."

What we already know about dolls of this type is that they were made in and exported from Europe, especially France, from about 1865 to 1880. What their clothes tell us is that they (more specifically, she) are dressed in a style introduced in about 1875, one that remained fashionable for some years thereafter. The family history is clearly inaccurate. The girl mentioned in the note was in all likelihood the mother of the child and was born, as the note indicates, in 1850. Her daughter received the dolls for her birthday, also as indicated, but in 1876, perhaps—certainly not in 1862!

Neither the bridal gown nor the wedding suit are commercially made dolls' garments, and yet they display more adeptness at stitchery than the ordinary doting mother might possess. Thus it can be assumed that these oufits display the skills of the local seamstress and tailor. Today, this pair of dolls tells us more about fashionable wedding clothes as worn in Maine in the late 1870's than any photograph, written de-

scription, drawing, or wedding gown preserved up in the attic,
because the garments have been preserved while actually being
worn by the dolls.

In the world of antiques, dolls are unique in that they form
an emotional link with the past. In *A Treasury of Beautiful
Dolls* this link has been reinforced through the illustrations.
Everyone with a feeling for beauty and charm will enjoy the
pictures of dolls in this volume. The color photographs were
especially commissioned, and the photographer, Peter Reinstorff, has admirably caught the personalities of the dolls,
whether they have a stately loveliness or a whimsical appeal.

Besides giving visual pleasure to a great many people, this
book demonstrates the importance of dolls from both the historical and the artistic points of view. It proves to the guardians
of both public and private collections the great importance of
keeping their dolls in as close to original condition as possible;
it especially emphasizes the necessity of preserving all original
clothes.

This is a totally new approach to antique dolls. Probably
no one else would be able to handle the task as successfully
and with such great sensitivity as has John Noble.

Dorothy, Elizabeth, and Evelyn Coleman

Acknowledgments

A book such as this calls for help from a great many people, and this book was fortunate indeed in having many wonderful friends.

I would like first to thank Peter Reinstorff and his assistants for their hard work, their imagination, and the results of their labors, the beautiful color plates in this book.

I am deeply grateful to the collectors who allowed me to invade their cabinets and conscript their treasured dolls for the color plates: Dorothy Blankley, Fanchon Canfield, E. J. Carter, Dorothy S., Elizabeth A., and Evelyn J. Coleman, Alberta Derby, Cora Ginsberg, Bess Goldfinger, Rebecca and Maureen Popp, Kit Robbins, and Margaret Whitton.

Some particular acknowledgments must be made here. Elizabeth Anne Coleman acted as chaperone for carloads of dolls from Washington and Maryland, chauffeuring them cheerfully to New York and attending to their welfare with professional care. Kit Robbins dove into her enviable archives to find rare prints and engravings, and she spent hours photographing her own dolls and the author's to provide black-and-white illustrations. During all the weeks of photography Margaret Whitton allowed us to use her house as a meeting place, studio, and restaurant, and a great deal of work we made for her; Blair Whitton met the repeated invasions of his home with hospitality and patience.

I would especially like to thank Bess Goldfinger publicly for her remarkable and touching generosity. The "Rose Pierrette" doll was a gift to me, made impulsively when I found it in her collection and raved over it.

The members of the Coleman family, besides lending their dolls and contributing their generous Foreword, were unstinting with their advice and knowledge, and they most kindly edited the manuscript.

I am deeply indebted to the doll clubs that have welcomed me to their meetings and allowed me to take pictures, especially the Doll Collectors Guild, the Dollology Club, of Washington, D. C., the Jenny Lind Doll Club, the Long Island Doll and Hobby Club, and the National Doll and Toy Collectors Club. To my good friends in these organizations, many, many thanks.

Without the Museum of the City of New York this would be a much slimmer volume; I am most grateful to the museum and its staff for its cooperation and for the use of its collections and archives.

Last but by no means least, my most sincere thanks to my companion, Father Robert Clement, for his support and encouragement, his patience, and his enthusiasm.

J. N.

Contents

Foreword
   by Dorothy, Elizabeth, and Evelyn Coleman vii
Acknowledgments xi
List of Color Plates xvii
List of Black-and-White Illustrations xix
Introduction xxiii
1. Georgian Splendor 1
2. Sense and Sensibility 13
3. American Primitives 31
4. Romantic Revival 45
5. Innocence and Bliss 53
6. Love in Wax 67
7. Oriental Attitudes 83
8. Ringlets and Ribbons 89
9. French Elegance 111
10. Children of Paris 125
11. German Inventions 139
12. American Classics 149
13. Rarities and Mysteries 171
14. Second Time Around 185
   Epilogue 203
   Index 207

Lists of Plates
and Illustrations

List of Color Plates

PLATE   1.   "Mary Jenkins," an English wooden doll, c. 1745   35

PLATE   2a. Wax doll, c. 1790   36

PLATE   2b. German wax dolls in an arbor, c. 1770   36

PLATE   3.   German papier-mâché dolls, c. 1820–1850   37

PLATE   4a. German papier-mâché dolls, c. 1830–1850   38

PLATE   4b. German pegwooden, dressed as a peddler, c. 1845   38

PLATE   5.   German pegwoodens, dressed as the Virgin Mary and attendant angels, c. 1825   39

PLATE   6.   American rag dolls, made by Izannah Walker, c. 1845–1875   40

PLATE   7.   German porcelain dolls, c. 1840   41

PLATE   8.   German china doll, perhaps a portrait of Fanny Elssler, c. 1844   42

PLATE   9.   German china dolls, c. 1850–1860   91

PLATE   10a. Rubber doll, c. 1870   92

PLATE   10b. German china children, c. 1860–1885   92

PLATE   11a. German and American papier-mâché dolls, c. 1845–1870   93

PLATE   11b. German *badekinder*, or bathing dolls, c. 1860   93

PLATE   12a. German wax baby, Motschmann type, c. 1855   94

PLATE   12b. "Charles," a German waxed–papier-mâché doll, c. 1865   94

PLATE   13.   English (?) poured-wax doll, c. 1870   95

PLATE   14a. English (?) poured-wax dolls, c. 1885–1890   96

PLATE   14b. German composition doll, c. 1875   96

PLATE   15a. German wax dolls, representing Orientals, c. 1860–1880   97

PLATE   15b. German bisque-headed baby doll, dressed as a Chinese temple-dancer, c. 1910   97

PLATE   16a. German bisque dolls, c. 1865–1875   98

PLATE   16b. German bisque dolls, called hooded chinas or fancies, c. 1890–1900   98

PLATE   17.   German fancy-bisque doll heads, c. 1870–1875   155

PLATE   18a. French china lady dolls, c. 1860   156

PLATE   18b. French china lady dolls, perhaps by Maison Huret, c. 1860   156

PLATE   19a. French bisque lady doll with articulated wooden body, c. 1875   157

xvii

PLATE 19b. French bisque lady dolls, c. 1870–1875   157

PLATE 20. French *bébés*, c. 1880   158

PLATE 21. French *bébés* Jumeau, c. 1890   159

PLATE 22. German bisque dolls by Heubach Brothers, c. 1905   160

PLATE 23. German clown dolls, c. 1900–1920   161

PLATE 24. American rubber-headed dolls, made by the
           India Rubber Comb Company, c. 1875   162

PLATE 25a. American wooden dolls, made by Albert Schoenhut,
            c. 1911   195

PLATE 25b. German-made bisque Kewpie dolls,
            c. 1913, © J.L.K.   195

PLATE 26a. "Bobby Bounce," an American composition doll,
            designed by Grace Drayton, c. 1910   196

PLATE 26b. "Gladdie," two versions of an American doll,
            designed by Helen Jensen, c. 1920   196

PLATE 27a. Waxed–papier-mâché doll with molded headdress   197

PLATE 27b. French *bébé* made by Maison Huret, c. 1885   197

PLATE 28. French mechanical doll, made by
           Alexandre Théroude, c. 1855–1860   198

PLATE 29. French and American dolls,
           representing Charlie Chaplin, c. 1910–1920   199

PLATE 30. French boudoir doll, c. 1925   200

PLATE 31a. English bisque doll, c. 1920   201

PLATE 31b. Boy doll with painted head, c. 1900–1910   201

PLATE 32. "Anne of Cleves," a bisque portrait doll
           by Martha Thompson, c. 1960   202

LIST OF BLACK-AND-WHITE ILLUSTRATIONS

An eighteenth-century engraving of little girls playing
    with their dolls   7

Family group by Anthony Devis, c. 1730   7

English wooden doll, early eighteenth century   8

"Mademoiselle Catherina," an engraving after a painting,
    early eighteenth-century   9

A fashionable portrait of the eighteenth century   9

Swaddled wax baby, late seventeenth century   10

Italian wax religious figure, eighteenth century   10

Wax dancing dolls from a music box, c. 1740   10

English wax doll, 1758   11

Christopher Anstey and his daughter, c. 1775   11

"Mary King," a Dutch carved wooden doll, c. 1805   12

German papier-mâché–headed doll, c. 1810   20

"Ladies of Distinction in Fashionable Dresses," an
    engraving of about 1808   21

A woodcut from *The Daisy*, 1808   21

A fashion plate of the late 1820's   22

A fashion plate from *La Belle Assemblée*, 1823   22

"Les Jouets du jour de l'an," a lithograph of 1824   23

"The Young Mother," an engraving of about 1828   24

Doll dressed in shellwork, late 1820's   24

German papier-mâché doll, c. 1835   25

Wooden dolls with molded plaster faces, c. 1830   26

Coiffures from a fashion plate of the 1830's   27

Small pegwooden dolls, c. 1830   28

Doll with papier-mâché head, c. 1850   29

"Girl in a Garden," c. 1840   30

"Baby with Doll," c. 1845   43

American rag doll made by Izannah Walker   44

American rag doll, maker unknown   44

"Mr. and Mrs. Charles Henry Carter," c. 1840   49

Fanny Elssler at the Park Theater, an engraving of 1840   50

Fanny Elssler as La Sylphide   51

"The Ernest Fiedler Family," 1850   58

Large china head, c. 1845   58

Two china dolls with inset glass eyes   59

Lithograph of a New York toyshop, 1865   60

A child with her china doll, a photograph of the 1860's   60

German china doll, c. 1870   61

China boy doll of the late 1870's   62

"Reading the News," a stereopticon card of the 1860's   62

"The House That Jack Built," an English set piece, c. 1875   63

A pair of small *badekinder*   63

A group of three small *badekinder*   64

German *badekind* made of rubber   65

Doll's head of hard rubber, c. 1875   65

Doll similar to that patented by Motschmann in 1857   73

"The Wilson Children," c. 1860   74

Waxed–papier-mâché doll   75

"Rough and the Doll," from *The Prize* magazine, 1886   75

German wax figurine, c. 1850   76

Small wax doll, c. 1850   76

American trade card, late 1870's   77

Doll with waxed composition head   77

English family photograph   78

Poured-wax doll dressed as a bride, c. 1885   78

Photograph of a child with her doll, c. 1885   79

Poured-wax–headed baby doll   79

Poured-wax doll, late 1880's   80

Christmas candy box in the shape of a doll   80

Waxed dolls in a state of "pleasing decay"   81

Two engravings of everyday life in China, published in
      London in 1812   86

Rockingham porcelain figure, c. 1830   86

"Tea and Coffee," a plate from *Les Fleurs animées,* 1847   87

Mechanical Chinaman doll, c. 1870   87

Four German bisque dolls with Oriental features, 1900–1920   88

A lithograph depicting a toy store, late 1890's   102

English porcelain fruit-dish by Minton, 1853   103

Small bisque doll, molded in one piece   103

Twin dolls with bisque heads, late 1870's   104

Bisque doll with elaborately decorated head   105

Boy doll, late 1870's   106

Bisque-headed doll, late 1870's   106

A late bisque doll with molded jewelry   107

Photograph of a lady of the 1870's   107

A late bisque with elaborate decorations   108

Head of a German bisque figurine, 1890's   108

Doll's head in coarse bisque, wearing a blossom as a hat   109

A group of so-called Marguerite dolls   109

German embossed "scraps" from the 1890's   110

French doll made by Maison Huret, 1860's   117

Fashion plate from *Le Moniteur de la mode*, 1856   117

French lady doll in elaborate dress   118

Two French fashion plates showing children with their dolls   119

French lady doll in summer costume, c. 1867   120

Plate of fashions for children, 1875   120

French lady doll representing a mulatto   121

French lady doll in Near Eastern costume   121

Fashion plate showing children in fancy dress, c. 1875   122

Two dolls dressed as bride and groom, c. 1875   123

"Wedding Presents," 1880   130

A *bébé* Bru in a late-1870's costume   131

Fashion plate from *Le Journal des enfants*, 1884   132

French fashion plate, 1880   133

Bébé with unmarked head, marked Jumeau body   134

A boy doll and his twin baby sisters, marked "Breveté"   134

French fashion plate of the 1880's   135

"Cornelia Ward Hall and Her Children," c. 1880   136

A *bébé* Jumeau, dressed as an Arab   137

German lady doll made by Simon and Halbig   144

German lady doll by Simon and Halbig, c. 1910   145

Marie Constable, a photograph of 1895   146

"The Children's Teaparty," a stereopticon card, 1900   146

A bisque shoulder-head by Simon and Halbig   147

"Baby," the famous character doll of Kammer and Reinhardt, 1909   147

Head of a laughing child, by Heubach Brothers   148

Doll's head made in the manner of the Heubach dolls   148

Schoenhut girl doll with molded hair   163

Head of a Schoenhut boy doll   163

xxi

Ringmaster doll, from a Schoenhut "Humpty Dumpty Circus"   164

A valentine by Ernest Nister, 1910   164

Kewpie valentines, c. 1918   165

Three Kewpie derivatives   166

A clock case in bisque, with dancing Kewpies   166

Kewpies designed to hold talcum powder   167

"Charlie Chaplin," a modern celluloid mechanical doll   167

"Charlie McCarthy," a ventriloquist's doll, c. 1935   168

"Jiggs," a doll based on a character from the comic strip
     "Bringing Up Father"   168

"W. C. Fields," portrait doll made by Effanbee, c. 1930   169

French Negro lady dolls   177

Two French dolls representing laughing Moors   178

Waxed–papier-mâché doll with molded hat, c. 1885   178

A mechanical toy, a variant on the Goodwin patent of 1868   179

A mechanical toy, made by Vichy, of Paris, in the 1850's   180

Unusual French mechanicals   181

German man doll with papier-mâché head and molded cap   182

French Jumeau doll dressed to represent Eleanor of Austria   183

"Mischief" and "Michael," bisque dolls made by Ellery Thorpe   189

"La Duchesse de Longeville," a portrait doll
     by Martha Thompson   190

A group of dolls by Martha Thompson, based on
     fashion plates of the 1830's   191

Fashion plate of a gentleman of the late 1820's   192

"Prince Albert of Saxe-Coburg," a portrait doll by
     Martha Thompson   193

A doll representing an old peasant woman, by Ada Odenrider   193

Introduction

Garden follies and grottoes, snuffboxes and shell work, gravestones and mourning jewelry, puppets, postcards, and Christmas-tree ornaments: From my earliest years such minor decorative arts have held an intense fascination, being as they are the offshoots, the outer edges, of aesthetic experience. The eccentric, the morbid, the frivolous and the trivial, the excessively familiar and therefore overlooked—they compel my attention and enthrall my mind.

Of all such delights, the beauty of old dolls is the quintessential one. It has distracted me for years, leading me down remote and dreamlike paths to the disparate places where old dolls are to be found, introducing me to rare, magic people. Of my diffuse interests among the minor arts, none has been so rewarding as this obsession with the beauty of dolls.

This book is not intended as a history nor as any kind of guide or textbook. It is an attempt to show the kaleidoscopic and seemingly infinite variety of dolls and to demonstrate how, as a microcosm, they reflect the vagaries of taste down through the years. This is a personal selection of a few dolls that have been carefully chosen from many available, and the author has had the rare pleasure of being guided by his preferences rather than by other considerations.

J. N.

"I belong to a race, the sole end of whose existence is to give pleasure to others. None will deny the goodness of such an end, and I flatter myself that we amply fulfill it. Few of the female sex especially but will acknowledge, with either the smile or the sigh called forth by early recollections, that much of their youthful happiness was due to our presence; and some will even go so far as to attribute to our influence many a habit of house-wifery, neatness and industry which ornaments their riper years. . . .

"Personal beauty I might almost, without vanity, call the 'badge of all our tribe.' Our very name is seldom mentioned without the epithet pretty; and in my own individual case I may say that I have always been considered pleasing and elegant, although others have surpassed me in size and grandeur."

—from *The Doll and Her Friends*, a children's book published in Boston in 1852

A Treasury
of
Beautiful Dolls

CHAPTER 1

Georgian Splendor

Most of the dolls chosen for this book are from the nineteenth and twentieth centuries. It may seem odd to confine the scope of a book deliberately, considering the range of the subject. Granting an initial decision to concentrate on dolls from our Western culture, surely there must be beautiful dolls made in earlier times?

There are indeed, but to identify them with confidence is not at all easy. A doll is a plaything, representing a human person, and when we speak of dolls, we are thinking of children's playthings. It is easy to say that children have always played with dolls, and that examples can be found among the relics of other and ancient cultures, but it is not at all easy to substantiate such a statement. We have only to go back two hundred years in our own culture to find that it is quite difficult to judge exactly what was or was not a child's toy, just as it is difficult to distinguish exactly who was a child.

Children as we know them today, sharply distinctive creatures who spend a golden decade in a specially organized wonderland before becoming "teen-agers," have existed for a comparatively short time and are essentially a nineteenth-

1

century concept. The children of earlier eras, even the little aristocrats, knew no such wonderland. Once babyhood was over, the boys were breeched, and along with their breeches came swords, which they were taught to use. After learning how to defend their property, they were trained to administer it. Many people were dependent upon a gentleman, and consequently he had much to learn and many duties to assume. His sisters were expected to make good marriages, and twelve years was not too early an age for a wedding ceremony. A lady had to acquire many accomplishments before that occasion in order to manage properly her future home.

Among the lower classes early life was even more grim: apprentices of tender years were overworked and underfed, tiny children slaved in mines, and country children worked equally hard. There is a pathetic account recorded in the 1830's of a tiny "scarecrow," left in the fields from dawn until dusk, alone, hungry, and frightened, singing in his quavering baby voice to keep up his spirits.*

While all these children accepted without demur responsibilities that we would today consider adult, their guardians were, paradoxically, far more childlike than it is possible to be in our culture, even if we dared. The privileged classes enjoyed a robust simplicity despite their book learning and their knowledge of the arts. They reveled in crude practical jokes, played simple games with gusto, and loved toys. Jumping jacks, diabolo, dollhouses, toy theaters, solitaire, spillikins—these and many other toys and games were at one time or another the fads of these adults. Thus it is not at all easy to take a doll of any great age, without documentation to help us, and to say with any authority: "This is a child's doll."

Before such statements can be made, much careful research is needed, demanding a book of its own—a fascinating and tempting project. Meanwhile it seems wiser to concentrate on dolls from the nineteenth century and after—dolls made primarily for children and from a background with which most of us are reasonably familiar.

* The "scarecrow story" was originally told in *The Boy's Country Book* by William Howett, published in England in the 1830's. The story and song are repeated in *When Victoria Began to Reign* by Margaret Lambert, pp. 147–149 (London: 1937).

In this chapter a few examples of eighteenth-century dolls are examined. They have been included here chiefly to acknowledge the sharp line drawn across history by the Industrial Revolution. They help to demonstrate simply the differences in dolls before and after the emergence of the German toy-making industry at the end of the eighteenth century and the different attitudes toward children.

The common doll of the eighteenth century was a wooden one—a remarkably crude affair, considering that it is found chiefly in aristocratic houses. The bulk of the dolls came from England, although manufacture has been traced to several European countries, including Austria, Switzerland, France, and Holland. Many of them are from the earlier decades of the eighteenth century, but a few are from the seventeenth century.

These wooden babies were not factory products. They were made by journeymen working either in their homes or, if itinerant, by the roadside. Often the dolls were a sideline to the manufacturer of more mundane artifacts. In the fascinating extract from *Sessions of the Peace* (1733), quoted by Alice Early in her book, *English Dolls, Effigies, and Puppets*, we catch a glimpse of the bustle and concerns of such a journeyman's household as well as a touching insight into the craftsman's pride in his work: "I am a turner by trade, but my chief business is to make babies. . . . I know my own babies from any other man's, [and] I can swear to my own work, for there's never a man in England that makes such babies besides myself."*

Dolls such as this were still being made as late as 1820, although by this time the competition from mass-produced dolls was almost overwhelming. It is difficult to date the wooden babies, since there are no patents, catalogs, or other dated documents, and since a healthy craftsman could have produced his own version of a doll over a period of forty years or so with very few variations once he had mastered his skills. Thus, if he were also itinerant, his distinctive doll could have been scattered over the English countryside in the space of more than a quarter of a century and might be found wearing the

* London: 1956, p. 90.

clothes of 1730 or 1770, both equally original. How is one to date such dolls?

Slowly, as the wooden babies changed, they deteriorated in quality. The earlier dolls are the finer ones. Into the roughly turned basic form their features were carved with a subtle awareness of personality and with remarkable vitality. As the century progressed the carving gradually become slicker and more competent and the heads more globular. Features became bunched and sharply linear, stylized from a set of three-dimensional planes into a graph.

The splendid early example in Plate 1 is very well documented. The doll was brought from England to New York in 1745 for a child named Mary Jenkins and was treasured by generations of the Jenkins family. The doll looks today exactly as she did when Mary Jenkins put her away; she has never been cleaned, repaired, or restored in any way.

The carving here is intensely personal and is done with consummate mastery. The forms are beautifully realized; the planes of the forehead, cheeks, and jaw are defined as deftly as in a sculpture by Aristide Maillol or a painting by Paul Cézanne. There is a penetrating exploration of personality. The doll stands as stately as a cathedral, although she is a mere eighteen inches high. Her hands rest serenely in her lap. One can compare her to a monolithic Mexican god or an Easter Island statue, and she will hold her own. This is the way she has always looked. The fadings and frayings of time do not dim her splendor but add mystery to her presence—the mystery that roses acquire when they are dried for potpourri.

Her dress reminds us of potpourri, with its withered brocades and faded colors: blue and fawn and pink and lemon. Like many of the dresses for these dolls, it is made of a formal patchwork, using the narrow strips of silk saved from the seam trimmings of grown-up dresses. These patchwork gowns are so ubiquitous as to imply an unwritten tradition. The extreme preciousness of the damasks and brocades would prohibit their squandering on a doll's dress—even of scraps and pieces if they were large enough to make a purse, line a box, or cover a book. This dress is made crudely enough to be the work of little Mary Jenkins herself. The stitches are huge and clumsy, and the skirt is lined with paper. The ornament of leaves and

4

tendrils is made from scraps of the dress silks; it is clumsy, painstaking, and very touching. This magnificent doll is from the Museum of the City of New York, where she is on permanent exhibition.

Wax dolls were also made for the eighteenth-century child. They were not as common as wooden ones, and they were decidedly more expensive. Wax-working was a flourishing occupation at this period, especially in the Catholic countries, where there was a great demand for religious figures of all sizes, both for churches and for private shrines. The German wax dolls of this period are often very similar in construction to the wax religious figures and were surely made by the same craftsmen. "Baby houses" were fashionable conceits, and many such German dolls found homes within their paneled walls.

The beautiful doll in Plate 2a is made very much in the manner of late eighteenth-century church figures: Like Miss Jenkins it was made by a craftsman with the most rarefied skills at his fingertips. This doll is only seven inches high. The body is a wire armature bound with strips of linen; the head and limbs are poured wax. The modeling is extremely sensitive, and the features are refined and delicate. The eyes are brown droplets of wax and the pale lashes are set in a strip into the modeled lids—a difficult task on such a small doll. The finely frizzled wig is pinned into position.

The dress of this doll, as one might expect, is exquisitely understated. A simple gown of ivory-colored silk is worn over a quilted silk petticoat. The low neckline is trimmed with gauze; the airy silk train that falls from her shoulders is a most delicate blue color. A fashionable apron of fine lace is bordered with silk chenille.

Everything about this little doll is consummately gracious, and it is all achieved with the lightness of touch and economy of means which are typical of its time. We are reminded of the late portraits of Thomas Gainsborough, all silvery dazzle, the light shimmering from one rich surface to another. This doll is from the Coleman collection.

Plate 2b shows two commercially made German wax dolls. Here they have been used as ornaments in a little decorative wax arbor made at home by the ladies of the house as a winter amusement. The arbor and dolls were probably preserved in a rosewood case or perhaps under a glass dome by the owners in the late eighteenth century. The Museum of the City of New York has a much earlier example of such a group, made by a New York child in the 1720's. The dolls in Plate 2b are constructed similarly to the handmade wax doll in Plate 2a, but the work here is much less fine. The eyes of the man are painted, whereas those of his lady are simple glass beads. The hair of both dolls is made of elaborately dressed and rigidly stiffened tow.

The costumes are from the 1770's; they are extremely fashionable, and the way in which they are made suggests that this work was done at home. The brocades have been chosen with care so that their sprigs and stripes are correctly scaled, and the gentleman's fine silk stockings have been minutely sewn to fit his spindly legs. The flowers and ribbons on the lady's elegant black hat are contrived from silver bullion and colored gauzes. Both costumes are decorated with gold and silver braid, chenille ruchings, and flowered ribbons.

The bower in which this bemused pair are seated is a very personal invention. The flowers that rampage up its latticed sides are by no means the hackneyed sprays one finds in the pattern books of the day. These are someone's favorite flowers: Yellow laburnum grows beside pink honeysuckle, a passion-flower keeps pace with a climbing apricot-colored rose, and jasmine and stephanotis are jostled by wild fuschias and clover-cops, all made by talented amateur hands.

The one thing that is not original is the lady's bouquet. It is made of wax orange-blossoms, the commercial kind worn by brides from about 1880 onward. It has been carefully and lovingly wired to the lady's wrist. This group is from the collection of Cora Ginsberg.

6

An eighteenth-century engraving of a group of little girls playing the timeless game of bathing and dressing their dolls, then putting them to bed. The children are finely dressed, and the dolls are quite elaborate. (*Kit Robbins Collection*)

Family group by Anthony Devis, c. 1730. This is the way English country gentlemen saw themselves: calm and tranquil, disposed with their family in a tasteful manner within a planned landscape. The doll "Mary Jenkins" would fit perfectly into this picture.

English wooden doll of the early eighteenth century, wearing a saque-backed dress of worsted-embroidered linen which opens over a quilted satin petticoat (*Jeremie Rockwell Gardiner Knott Collection*)

"Mademoiselle Catherina," an early-eighteenth-century engraving from an original painting in Vauxhall Gardens. Mlle. Catherina appears to be a mechanical walking or dancing doll of the kind popular as children's toys a century later. (*Kit Robbins Collection*)

A fashionable portrait from the early eighteenth century, demonstrating the valued points of beauty: the oval face, almond eyes, bland expression, and long, swanlike neck. All these features are further exaggerated in the wooden dolls.

9

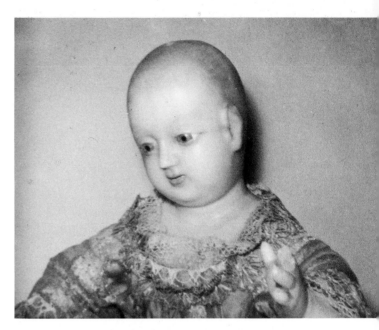

Swaddled wax baby, late seventeenth century
(Kit Robbins Collection)

Italian wax religious figure, eighteenth century
(Kit Robbins Collection)

Two small solid-wax dancing dolls, mounted on bristles, from a music box, c. 1740 *(Kit Robbins Collection)*

10

English wax doll, wearing, according to its label, which is in the original owner's writing, a "long robe coat, full dress for a lady of sixteen," 1758 (Bethnel Green Museum, London)

Christopher Anstey and his daughter, painted by William Hoare. The doll appears to be a wax one. Her fantastic towering coiffure was in fashion in the mid-1770's. (National Portrait Gallery, London)

"Mary King," a carved wooden doll brought from Holland to New York in 1805 by Rev. Joseph King for his daughter Mary and redressed by her in 1846 for her niece, Mary King Murray, at which time the beautiful straw bonnet was made, obviously by a professional milliner. The flame-stitch purse was stitched for the doll by this second owner, and the little beaded moccasins were a gift from Indian admirers who befriended the same child and her doll during a visit to Canada. *(Museum of the City of New York)*

CHAPTER 2

Sense and Sensibility

The title of the famous novel by Jane Austen aptly describes the curious little dolls portrayed in plates 3 and 4a. They contrast greatly with the aristocratic toys that we have already examined. These dolls were intended for a very different market, and they are thoroughly commercial in concept.

The first mass-produced molded–papier-mâché heads of this kind had been introduced at Sonneberg, Thuringia, in the early years of the nineteenth century, a time when the long-established but insular German toy trade was expanding to embrace a world market. These early heads are outstanding. They are beautifully modeled and conceived with great vitality, deriving in style and manner from the classical ideals of the late eighteenth century. These early examples have been largely neglected by collectors simply because there are so few of them that they are virtually unknown to many people.

Most decorative objects that are in production over a long period of time have "careers" that can be divided into clearly defined stages. The objects of the first, or pioneer, stage express new ideas and perhaps exploit new processes; they are always vivid and exciting. In the next phase the most successful and efficient of the variants reach prominence. At this point the objects acquire their distinctive characters and achieve the peak of their success—still fresh and original. In the third stage the objects become classics and sometimes even cliché. Finally there is decadence: The products are either drained of vitality through overproduction, or else they are cheapened in an effort to hold the market.

By the 1820's the papier-mâché dolls had evolved into an economical and practical product, the body made simply and durably from two strips of stitched and stuffed kid, the wooden limbs partially fashioned by lathe. The three rare and lovely dolls in Plate 3 are typical, and the lady dolls especially are good examples of the larger sizes and fresh, lively modeling which characterize the earlier dolls of this type. Both have their original clothing, complete and undisturbed.

The lady on the left has the formal features and the smooth, columnlike neck which are derived from classical sculpture. Her fashionable coiffure is a style based on Roman portraits. The beguilingly simple dress is printed cotton with a faded pink pattern, and the painted shoes are rose-colored. The clothes are typical of the middle of the decade, although the very short skirt and plainly visible pantaloons suggest a young girl rather than an adult.

The lady on the right has a most unusual head, with delicate, subtly modeled features. Her coiffure is graced with a braided knot high up on the crown. The contemporary straw bonnet came with the doll, but it is oddly in conflict with the hairstyle, which requires one of the specifically designed high-crowned hats of the period. The bonnet does not sit comfortably and leads one to wonder wistfully if there was once a second, sister doll. Her dress is silk gauze mounted on fine pink silk. The sash is made of the clearer-pink satin of the bonnet ribbons and is edged with blond. Again, the pantaloons show that this is a girl's dress. The shoes here are viridian-colored. Both dolls are from the collection of Margaret Whitton.

The gentleman doll is very unusual. He is more difficult to date than the ladies but probably was made between 1820 and 1850. The distinctly childlike head with its set-in glass eyes is most unusual for this period and is not typical of this type of

14

doll; one would question it, were it not that the shoulders of the coat, undoubtedly original, fit with precision over the doll's shoulder plate. The suit is a fashionable bottle-green color, with a dark-velvet collar and brass buttons. The careful details of his costume, the nicety of his linen, and the accurate disposition of his pockets add much to the charm of this little gentleman. He possesses a towering beaver hat, which completes the correct silhouette of the late-Georgian dandy. It was regretfully left out of the picture because it is sadly battered and unphotogenic and also in order to show the head of this rare doll, with its distinctive painted hair arranged *en coups de vent* —the proper Romantic manner. He has clearly had his anachronistic real-gold watch-chain (revealingly called an albert in England) for a long time. In his heyday he would of course, have sported a fob, but the chain speaks clearly of affection bestowed at a later date, and one is delighted to see it left undisturbed. This fine doll is from the collection of Dorothy Blankley.

These beautiful papier-mâchés continued to be made in great quantities until the middle of the century and were increasingly popular, to judge from the very large numbers of the later examples which have come down to us. With their dainty sizes, their lightness and delicacy, and their precise and intense romanticism, these dolls speak eloquently of the taste of their times. There had been growing up in Europe a prosperous middle class, in which were fused the second generation of the new industrialists with the lower echelons and poor relations of the old aristocracy. The novels of Jane Austen give us an insight into the ways of the middle class and its limitations. Her works contain no hint of the dissolute splendors of the court or of concern with war and political crises, although she was writing at one of the crucial periods in English history. Her boundaries were prescribed; she wrote for gentlefolk.

Our little dolls were intended for this middle-class market, and for Plate 4a a group of them have been chosen to show a panorama of the changing styles and characters of the years 1830 to 1850. In spite of great differences in mood, these dolls are above all genteel, and they invariably represent fashionable and soigné ladies and young girls.

The 1830's saw the desire for gentility and refinement reach the intensity of a cult. The inverted snobbery of dowdiness, the vulgarity of money, and the coarseness of physical functions (even eating) are brilliantly satirized in Miss Mitford's *Cranford*. Paradoxically, this decade saw the full flowering of the Romantic Revival, and fashionable costumes achieved an outrageous eccentricity that was not matched until the early 1900's. In the second doll from the left of our picture, these two contradictory elements meet: The coiffure with its towering loops and braids and jutting masses of curls is the peak of sophistication, whereas the dress is homemade and demure The doll in the dark dress is a little earlier and is much more restrained. The unusual head combines painted hair with real curls; this doll is serene and dignified. By the 1840's both the dignity and the panache have been subdued, and the two examples here—the dolls at the extreme left and right of the photograph—although extremely pretty, are nevertheless abashed and self-effacing. These are perhaps the most lovely dolls of this group; their elaborate dresses are original and undisturbed, and their calm, gentle features are as fresh as when they were first painted.

Much of the vigor and vitality had faded by the 1850's, and although the dolls of this date are plentiful, they tend to be monotonous and uninspired. The number of large-sized dolls, as seen in the doll in the pale dress, suggests that they no longer reflected the spirit of the age, which was neat, small, exquisite, and ladylike. The smaller late doll here, in the center of the group, is an enchanting and vivacious exception.

A curious social comment is provided by the little Negro doll in the foreground. Of the same period (about 1840) and structure, it has ethnically accurate features, and although it is not unique, it is extremely rare. The oddness of this doll—its startling difference from almost all the others of its kind—bring many questions to mind. Some of them are answered by the provenance of this doll; with a similar companion she was placed in a New York dollhouse in the 1840's as a servant.

The doll in the bonnet (on the left) and the three dolls in the right foreground are from the collection of E. J. Carter. The rest are from the Museum of the City of New York.

Even more popular in the early nineteenth century were

16

the little wooden dolls made on the same scale, which have been appropriately named pegwoodens by collectors. They are a part of the enchanting microcosm formed by the toys made in the cottages of the Groder Thal, in Germany, from the late eighteenth century onward. It is a microcosm of peasant simplicity and peasant splendor, a reflection of the insular life-styles of its creators, curiously stilted but perfectly serious and evolved with such conviction and vivacity that it was to have an immense influence on children everywhere for over a century.

As late as the 1930's its spirit was still very much alive, especially in the field of children's literature. Florence K. Upton's book *The Adventures of Two Dutch Dolls* and Frances Hodgson Burnett's *Racketty-Packetty House* were both written in the early 1900's, and both take place in this make-believe world. H. G. Hulme Beaman's "Toytown" stories came later, in the 1920's, and they achieved a special immortality in Britain when they were serialized for the B.B.C.'s *Children's Hour;* they are still being cherished after fifty years of radio broadcasting. The make-believe environment created in the mountain villages so long ago is powerful indeed.

Among the old surviving pegwooden dolls, again we find that the earliest are the finest. The wood is smooth and well seasoned, the jointing precise, the limbs articulated with beautiful ball-and-socket joints that permit a great deal of natural movement. The initial lathe turning was finished with careful hand carving. Faces, hair, and lower limbs were painted with flat colors and then thickly varnished, giving a translucent finish that becomes very mellow and beautiful with time.

The pegwoodens were cheap and plentiful and by the 1820's had reached a level of smooth excellence that was to last until the midcentury. They were the everyday dolls for little girls on both sides of the Atlantic. The efficient processes of the craftsmen acted like a machine to standardize them; their variety and charm derive largely from the imagination and care with which they were dressed. Hundreds of little girls learned their sewing skills by making clothes for them. Kate Greenaway describes in her writings her own childish delight in the family of pegwoodens which she collected and dressed when she was small, imbuing them with life and character. The little Princess Victoria, secluded in Kensington Palace, created a whole wonderland of glittering aristocrats and ballet dancers; the collection was preserved by Her Majesty with nostalgic care and in her old age was presented to the British nation.

Commercially dressed pegwoodens are rare. Presumably they were such an inexpensive product that costuming of any sort was impractical. They were, however, occasionally incorporated into toys made elsewhere. Some were used to populate the fantastic little grottoes of shells or minerals which, under their glass domes were popular parlor ornaments in the early nineteenth century.

In Plate 5 we find a very rare example of commercially dressed pegwoodens. Originally the Virgin Mary, her attendant angels, and a little home shrine were contained in a shadow box. The shrine itself was still extant the last time the dolls changed hands, but eventually it collapsed and was ruined beyond redemption. It was, of course, a glimpse of the Groder Thal wonderland; some hint of it is provided in the picture, which shows trees and fences from a toy of the same origin.

These particular pegwooden dolls are beautifully constructed: They are slender, smooth, and small (the Virgin is nine inches high). Made in the late 1820's, they seem to have been chosen with care for their dignified bearing and serene expressions. The silks and brocaded satins of their costumes are arranged exquisitely, the decorations being carried out both with bullion work and with tinsels exactly like those made to decorate English theatrical prints. The Virgin's high crown is made of embossed metallic paper. This material, along with the thin, papery satins, was to become part of the standard range of materials used commercially for costuming toys—particularly mechanical ones—for the rest of the century. (The dress of the Oriental mechanical in Plate 28 is a tour de force in this manner.)

The angels are charmingly stylized and wear the *tonnelet* used in romantic ballet costume.* Their slippers with fashion-

---

* The *tonnelet* was a stiffened skirt worn by male dancers in masques and ballets at the court of Louis XIV. Loosely based on the Roman tunic, it became a stylized costume, as did the later tulle skirt of lady dancers.

able crisscross ribbons are especially endearing, as are their stiff wings made—as dressmakers say—from self-material. This little group is immaculate and sparkling thanks to the defunct shadow box that protected it for nearly a century and a half. The pegwoodens are from the collection of Bess Goldfinger.

Plate 4b shows a pegwooden dressed as a peddler-woman in her traditional scarlet cloak and black bonnet. Such women were a common sight in England in the first half of the nineteenth century, trudging over the countryside among a motley company of itinerants, carrying all manner of trivial wares to remote rural districts. These peddler dolls were parlor ornaments and are often found complete with their glass domes or cases. Many of them were made at home and demonstrate great ingenuity, but a surprising number were commercial products. The charm of these dolls is in the astonishing detail with which their minute wares were fashioned and in their apparently infinite variety.

Unfortunately, these pretty ornaments caught the fancy of doll collectors in the early days of this hobby, when dolls were still considered frivolous trifles, and were subjected to liberties that no responsible collector would take today. Many fine peddler dolls were tampered with in the 1920's and 1930's, objects hopefully of the right period being added to enrich their baskets. One can often spot these objects—the glass jug made much too late, the fresh-cut edges on tiny leather gloves, or the beaded ornaments sewn with the wrong thread.

The lovely peddler in Plate 4b has happily been spared such vandalism. She and her wares are neat and orderly, exactly as they were first assembled in the late 1840's. This is a fine example of an elaboration on the classic pegwooden where the face and head are molded in plaster over a wooden core. This allows for beautifully detailed hairstyles and soft, naturalistic features reminiscent of the papier-mâché heads that we examined earlier.

The wares in her basket are in pristine condition and are a delight to explore. Notice the papers of straight pins, the card of tiny buttons, the "fine-comb" and the toothbrush, the pair of jet bracelets. There are enchantingly perfect knitted objects as well as an absurd mock-ermine tippet. The peddler-woman is from the collection of Margaret Whitton.

Unusually large, this magnificent German papier-mâché–headed doll
(c. 1810) is thirty-three inches high. The coiffure is sober and classic,
and the Greco-Roman influence on the sculptor is unmistakable.
(Maureen Popp Collection)

"Ladies of Distinction in Fashionable Dresses," an engraving of about 1808. The classical influence is still very strong, although it does not extend to the child's costume, which is already Romantic. (*Kit Robbins Collection*)

A woodcut from *The Daisy*, a child's book printed by Jacob Johnson, of Philadelphia, in 1808. The setting is pastoral and simple. The mother, although a lady, is of modest means. The toys, of commerical manufacture, are not precious. (*Author's Collection*)

A fashion plate of the late 1820's. The striking coiffure is in essence the same as that worn by the doll on the right in Plate 3. (Author's Collection)

A fashion plate from *La Belle Assemblée* for 1823. This coiffure is a much-decorated version of that worn by the doll on the left in Plate 3. (Author's Collection)

"Les Jouets du jour de l'an," a French lithograph of 1824. The toys are surprisingly large and numerous for the period. The doll with the "carton" (or cardboard) head and fashionable clothes is as tall as the child herself. (*Kit Robbins Collection*)

23

"The Young Mother," an engraving of about 1828. We notice that although the doll has the head of an adult, it wears the same child's dress as its "mother," a curious discrepancy that can often be found among the real dolls of the period. (*Kit Robbins Collection*)

Doll with papier-mâché head, elaborately dressed in shell-work. The dress is in the fashion of the late 1820's. Such dolls were popularly made at home and served as parlor ornaments; the example here, however, seems to be commercially made. (*The Shell Museum, Glandford, England*)

German papier-mâché doll, c. 1835, from the family of the Brett doll-house. The dress is fine silk-and-wool gauze. (*Museum of the City of New York*)

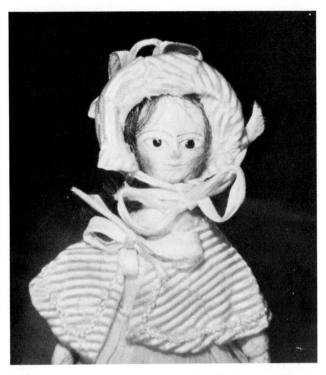

Two wooden dolls with molded plaster faces. Dolls of this type have long been considered eighteenth-century dolls and have optimistically been dated even earlier. They are in fact the factory-made version of the old wooden dolls and were evolved quite late in the eighteenth century. Examples from the 1830's, like the two dolls shown here, are by no means uncommon. *(Kit Robbins and Grace Ziebarth Collections)*

Ten variations on the elaborate towering coiffures of the 1830's, taken from a fashion plate of the day. The plates are scrupulously detailed but can only tell us how the hair looked from the front. To understand these remarkable structures fully, as well as to receive their full impact, we must turn to the contemporary papier-mâché dolls' heads. (*Author's Collection*)

Small pegwooden dolls, with painted yellow combs in their hair, c. 1830. The large doll is dressed as a child, whereas her own doll, oddly enough, is dressed as an adult. Present whereabouts unknown.

A late example of a papier-mâché head, perhaps from the 1850's. The interesting element here is the homemade body, very much too large in proportion, which gives an immensely dignified, monumental quality. This disproportion happens too often to be dismissed as clumsiness or lack of skill; comparisons with folk paintings of the time will show the same effect. This doll, happily, has not been altered, and the homemade costume is fascinating. The beaded purse and the apron, with its specially printed pattern, are most felicitous. (*McDonald Archive, Museum of the City of New York*)

"Girl in a Garden," c. 1840, artist unknown. Here is the same monumental quality that we found in the papier-mâché–headed doll shown on page 29. The child stands her ground as firmly as does architecture. *(Colonial Williamsburg)*

CHAPTER 3

American Primitives

The dolls pictured in Plate 6 were made by Izannah Walker, a Rhode Island spinster, during the third quarter of the nineteenth century. There is good reason to believe that they are the first original commercial dolls made in America. Because of their great beauty as well as their extraordinary background, it was decided to give them a chapter of their own instead of including them with the dolls discussed in Chapter 12, "American Classics."

Tantalizingly little is known about the maker of these American primitives; what is known is mostly hearsay, taken from the statements of a grandniece, Mrs. Norman Robertson, which were published by Janet Johl in her book *Your Dolls and Mine.** Family recollections are notoriously elastic, and Mrs. Robertson's fascinating accounts, which seem to have been handed down from her mother, are richly descriptive but often puzzlingly inconsistent when it comes to facts. For instance, she gives four different dates for the first doll and two different death dates for Izannah Walker. Although her factual

* New York: H. L. Lindquist, 1952.

evidence seems cloudy and unreliable, Mrs. Robertson's family history is nevertheless invaluable in that it provides us with a very vivid impression of Izannah Walker herself. She was clearly a remarkable character. According to Mrs. Robertson's account, which was published in a Rhode Island newspaper:

> Aunt Izannah always deplored the fact that she was not a man. However, she made dolls and dolls' furniture, tinkered with household gadgets, designed a parlor heater that "beat Ben Franklin's," raised canaries, dabbled in real estate, and was looked upon with admiration by male contemporaries because of her skill with carpenter's tools, so perhaps she was resigned.

Izannah Walker was born, according to Mrs. Robertson, in 1817, and she began making her dolls in the 1840's. They were patented in the summer of 1873 as "rag dolls." Their heads, which are painted with oil colors, are enchantingly simple and primitive-looking, although they are surprisingly complicated in design. Layers of glued cloth were pressed between two pairs of dies for the front and back of the head. When the shells so formed were dry and hard, they were thinly covered with cotton batting and then with pasted stockinette, after which they were replaced in the dies and pressed again. The resultant forms were stitched and glued together, and the head was ready to be stuffed and painted. The padded layer acts as a buffer that protects the painted surface. It also gives the heads their curious vibrancy, since the surface is yielding, like firm child's flesh. It is this secondary-layering process that is protected by the 1873 patent.

Such a doll was not invented overnight, and Mrs. Robertson tells of the struggles to perfect the layering process, including a charming story of the long wrestle with the problem of keeping the surface of the stockinette stiff enough to hold the paint without cracking. This problem was solved abruptly when Aunt Izannah, in bed one night, sat up suddenly to hear a voice commanding ex cathedra, "Use paste."

As the Colemans gently point out in their entry on the

32

Walker dolls in their *Collector's Encyclopedia of Dolls*,* however, to be legally valid a patent claim must be made for a product within two years of its appearance on the market. This means that the Walker dolls could not have been for sale publicly before 1871.

This is considerably different from the date the family gives, and although such discrepancies are common, thirty years is too disquieting a difference to ignore. In the absence of further facts we turn to the dolls themselves to seek the explanation.

The dolls are smooth and competently made, and their elaborate technical structure was certainly not evolved overnight. There must surely have been long and discouraging trial and error as well as many other voices in the night before the beautiful dolls that we know today were perfected. Thus Izannah could very well have been making dolls in the 1840's which were not these dolls. Also, one must remember that Central Falls, Rhode Island, in the mid-nineteenth century was no metropolis. The eccentric Miss Walker might well have perfected her dolls and for years have made them happily for relatives, neighbors, and perhaps church bazaars long before anyone took them seriously enough to encourage her to patent them.

There is a third explanation of this time discrepancy if the first two seem too weak to be valid. Dies are quite expensive things to have made, and Izannah had several sets, as can be seen by the variety of dolls depicted here. These dies would have had to be made early in the dolls' careers, and it is perfectly plausible that no one would have thought it necessary to change them. Children's toys have a tendency to ossify and become classic; there are china dolls and wooden toys which were made in Germany unchanged for at least sixty years and which were accepted without question by shopkeepers and children alike.

To Americans today, the Walker heads recall the styles of the 1840's and 1850's, but we must remember that our ideas of any nineteenth-century period are based on the styles of

* Dorothy S., Elizabeth A., and Evelyn J. Coleman (New York: Crown, 1968).

Paris and London. Even smart New Yorkers used to feel that their Paris dresses were too fashionable and put them away for two years until New York had "caught up." Central Falls, as we have suggested, was not a very sophisticated place, and in the 1870's there were doubtless many little girls in similar small towns whose clothes and hair resembled those of the Walker dolls enough for the dolls to be acceptable, if not the last word in style. So it could very well be that many of the Izannah Walker dolls that survive today were produced in the 1870's from dies that were made ten or twenty years earlier.

The superb group of Izannah Walker dolls in Plate 6 is from one collection, and it was a great privilege to be allowed to photograph them. Their "family" likeness is unmistakable, and yet each doll has a distinct character and is uniquely and intensely alive. Not only does each doll have its own die but also the treatment of the hair, the colors used, and the mood of the painting are individual to each of them. These are the creations of a dedicated craftsman, works of art of no small order.

Their bodies are as varied as their faces; their hands and feet are hand-modeled and -stitched, as are their delicate applied ears. The lower limbs are beautifully painted; some dolls have bare feet with deftly stitched toes, and others have shoes with painted laces. There is an unsubstantiated theory among collectors that the bare feet are earlier, and the owner of this group confirms that she has never seen a labeled Walker with bare feet. The effect of the patented process can clearly be seen. The curiously lifelike flesh is as yielding and vibrant as a ripe peach, a quality possessed by no other doll.

The two dolls in the bottom left-hand corner of Plate 6 have the patent label, proving that they were made after 1873. They shake our theories, so confidently stated earlier in this chapter, for they are quite different from the other dolls. The modeling is vaguer, the eyes are painted with insistence but less assurance, and there is a conscious striving after naturalism. As so often happens, when we have tried rationally to solve enigmas, the dolls themselves, bland and serene, confound us. This group of dolls is from the collection of Maureen Popp.

34

Plate 1. "Mary Jenkins," an English wooden doll, c. 1745

Plate 2a. Wax doll, c. 1790

Plate 2b. German wax dolls
in an arbor, c. 1770

Plate 3. German papier-mâché dolls, c. 1820–1850

Plate 4a.
German papier-mâché dolls,
c. 1830–1850

Plate 4b. German pegwooden,
dressed as a peddler, c. 1845

Plate 5. German pegwoodens,
dressed as the Virgin Mary and attendant angels, c. 1825

Plate 6. American rag dolls,
made by Izannah Walker, c. 1845–1875

40

Plate 7. German porcelain dolls, c. 1840

Plate 8. German china doll,
perhaps a portrait of Fanny Elssler, c. 1844

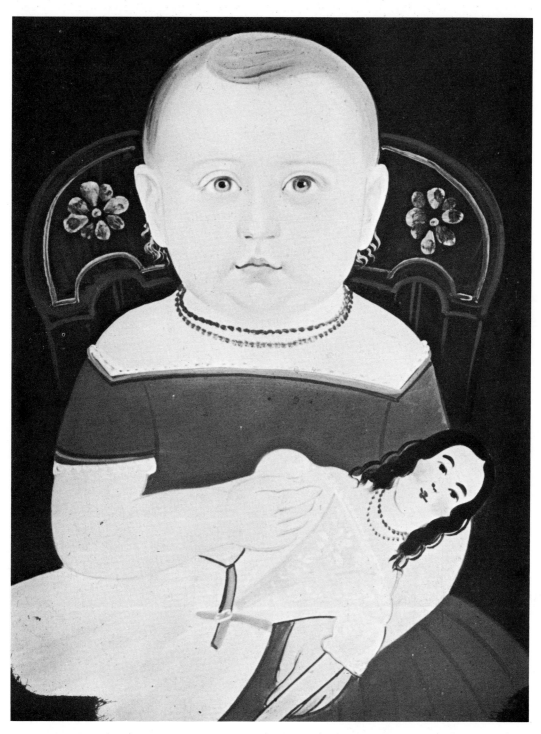

"Baby with Doll," attributed to Sturtevant J. Hamblin, c. 1845. This American primitive painting has affinities with the dolls of Izannah Walker, both in the way in which the child is perceived and also in the manner of handling the actual brushwork. (*Colonial Williamsburg*)

An Izannah Walker doll stands serenely alone to show her height, her printed-calico dress, and her charmingly simple hairstyle. (*Museum of the City of New York*)

A homemade rag doll from the same general place and time as those of Izannah Walker, and very much in the same manner. The craftswoman here, however, possessed limited skills. (*Kit Robbins Collection*)

CHAPTER 4

Romantic Revival

The atmosphere of the 1840's is a curiously complex one, and it is not easy to define in concise terms. In contrast with the preceding decades the 1840's are subdued and dove-colored. There is a sense of determined domesticity, of entrenchment, of taking the time to consolidate new powers or to recoup recent losses. The newly wed Queen Victoria of England has become the symbol of this decade, and indeed, she spent it most domestically, filling her palaces with nurseries. It was into this quiet, rather dowdy atmosphere, which pervaded most of Western Europe, that the early porcelain dolls made their debut.

The history of the beginnings of the commercial china dolls (which are such typical mid-nineteenth-century objects) is surprisingly vague. Little is known, and one can only point to the dolls as they appear on the scene. During the 1840's we find a number of superb porcelain dolls, sometimes with beautiful matching limbs. They are mostly unmarked, but they are works of a very high order, and on the rare occasions when a factory can be identified, we are not surprised to find it is a famous one. The Royal Berlin Porcelain Factory as well as the

Royal Factory of Copenhagen made a wide variety of dolls that are clearly marked. There are several other distinguishable manufacturers, and one hopes that research will in time shed more light on them.

The dolls in Plate 7 are excellent examples of these rare porcelain aristocrats. The lady is marked with a symbol, the initials "IH" in green, but although several other dolls are known that bear this mark, it tells us nothing about the manufacturer and may in fact be the initials of the painter, having no bearing on the factory.

The china is extremely fine, and the coloring is soft and gentle. The naturalism of the heads is immediately noticed; the lady is neither young nor pretty in any conventional sense. Her bones are aristocratic, her features delicate, and with her narrow chin and long, full upper lip, she seems to have been modeled from life. This lady is a mature adult, and her serene dignity is conveyed with a masterly economy of means.

The young gentleman is made of a different china and is realized with a different degree of realism. Again, the characterization is very distinctive. He has the barely formed bones and long neck of an adolescent; his features, however, are manly and sensitive, and he has a faraway, dreamy look, achieved also with remarkable economy and ease.

His costume is enchanting; it has the panache that was rapidly disappearing from men's clothes and would soon be discovered only among the uniforms of the soldiery. His linen is exquisitely finished, and his lilac waistcoat matches his heavy plush collar. As we look at him, we remember the less sober and dowdy aspects of the decade—Paris and "*la vie de bohème*," Gavarni and gala nights at the Opéra, Frédéric Chopin and Franz Liszt, and the mellow gleam of the haute monde. Both dolls are from the collection of Margaret Whitton.

In the past the identification of anonymous dolls as portraiture has been made too lightly, so that today's collector is faced with a profusion of "portraits": royalty, singers, president's wives. Factual proof of identity exists for very few of them. I do not wish to discuss here the origin of these dolls but instead an unusual instance in which circumstances are inverted. In this instance we have documentary evidence that a

46

specific portrait doll was made and the appearance of a doll
with a remarkably valid claim to that distinction.

It is recorded that at the Berlin Exhibition of 1844 a doll made by Aug. Poppe and intended to be a portrait of Fanny Elssler, the famous ballerina, was displayed. This record is particularly exciting, since true portrait dolls are very rare indeed, especially from these earlier decades. When they do occur, it is often because they were specifically made for an occasion such as this exhibition in Berlin.

Fanny Elssler was one of the three great ballerinas of the decade, and she was also one of the ballet's most vivid personalities, noted for her remarkable personal beauty. Théophile Gautier, describing her, says:

> She is tall, supple, and well-formed. . . . Mlle. Elssler is endowed with superb hair which falls on each side of her temples, lustrous and glossy as the two wings of a bird; the dark shade of hair clashes in too southern a manner with her typically German features; it is not the right head for such a body. This peculiarity is very disturbing and affects the harmony of the whole; her eyes, very black, the pupils of which are like two little stars of jet set in a crystal sky, are inconsistent with the nose, which, like the forehead, is German.*

With these words in mind, turn to the prints of Fanny Elssler on pages 50 and 51 to form an impression of her beauty.

In Plate 8 we find a doll unlike any other we have seen. It represents a dancer of the Romantic ballet and was made without question in the 1840's. The body has been carefully constructed, the long legs with their tapering calves and their feet *en pointe* are delicately carved of wood, and the silk tights are carefully fitted and sewn. The stitched kid hands with long, tapering fingers are very expressive. The china head seems small in proportion and is balanced on the long, thick, graceful neck and full shoulders. The face is strikingly alive

* Théophile Gautier, quoted in Sacheverell Sitwell, *The Romantic Ballet* (London: Batsford, 1948), p. 3.

and not in the least conventional. The features are tight and clearly realized: the eyes close set and brilliant, the forehead high and wide, the nose definite. Altogether, the face departs so far from both the accepted canons of beauty of the 1840's and from the canons of doll-making that we might indeed suppose that this is a special doll and an attempt, within the stylized terms of the medium, at portraiture.

It cannot be claimed, without further evidence, that this is Aug. Poppe's Fanny Elssler doll, but the possibility adds to our pleasure as we view this unique and most enviable of dolls. This doll is from the collection of Bess Goldfinger.

"Mr. and Mrs. Charles Henry Carter," attributed to Nicholas Biddle Kittell, c. 1840. Here is domestic bliss, the young husband quiet and studious, his wife gentle and devoted. Their parlor has the intensity and certainty of a dollhouse, its simple elegance greatly enriched by the brilliance of the colors. Nothing is done in this house without deliberation; when there is a child, its doll will be chosen with the same care. (*Museum of the City of New York*)

Fanny Elssler in her dressing room at the Park Theater, New York City, an engraving published in 1840. Her face, though stylized, has decided character, and a comparison with that of the doll in Plate 8 is interesting. (*George Chaffee Collection*)

Fanny Elssler as La Sylphide (*Museum of the City of New York*)

CHAPTER 5

Innocence and Bliss

The German china doll, like her wax sister, was a typical product of the nineteenth century. She arrived to stay in the late 1840's, evolving as a thoroughly commercial product and perhaps independently of the aristocratic dolls, some of which we have just examined, made a little earlier by very reputable china factories. Once established, these German china dolls were made in great quantities for at least ninety years, the style and merit of the different specimens varying greatly.

The early Victorian ideals were respectability and security, and domestic bliss was apparently the peak of aspiration. The home was the shrine, and Papa the high priest. As that security was achieved, the culture began to flower, the repressive atmosphere relaxed a little, and we find by midcentury a slowly blossoming effulgence—a world, on the surface at least, of lightness and delicacy. There was also a curious, earnest innocence, suspiciously like a deliberate blindness, as the comfortable middle classes continued to avoid the pressing social problems that followed prosperity. Gazing firmly in the other direction, they repeated the favorite maxim: "Distance lends enchantment to the view."

Reflections of this social level and its attitudes can be found in Plate 9, in which a group of china dolls of the period is posed for the camera. These ladies are very quiet and serene, with their still, classical features, their hair disposed modestly but with decision. There is no uncertainty here; to be beautiful, noses must be straight, and eyes are best blue. The embodiment of this closely prescribed ideal of beauty, further formalized by the restrictions of the medium, gives these dolls a considerable aesthetic potential. Additional restraints imposed on ther design include their being turned out in large quantities and at reasonable prices. Perhaps this is why they so often achieve a higher aesthetic standard than most of the costly china figurines of the period, where greater technical freedom allowed for more naturalism.

There are many subtle differences in the modeling, color, and brushwork of these apparently similar dolls. Serious research on them is just beginning, but it is already possible to identify the work of several different manufacturers by their distinctive qualities. On the other hand, they have a great deal in common, as can be seen by studying the plate. They gaze pensively back, facing us squarely, secure in their own quiet world. These dolls are from the collection of Margaret Whitton.

Dolls made from organic materials acquire aesthetic virtues of their own. The carved wooden dolls are a good example; so are those molded in rubber or gutta-percha and those of the strangely beautiful, translucent rawhide.

The head of the doll in Plate 10a is made of rubber in a pale sand color. The features and the simply arranged hair are sensitively modeled, and the restrained, stylized coloring enhances the delicate features without obliterating them. When the rubber was new, it was soft and pliant, and at that time the doll must have been a cosy, companionable creature.

Today, with the natural hardening and shrinking of the rubber, she has acquired a static quality, a monumental serenity that, by a happy chance, finds immediate echoes in the simplicity of her dress. Made at home in the 1870's, the woolen dress with its velvet trim now has a rubbed patina that complements the finely withered surface of the ancient rubber, and the beautiful faded blue is in perfect harmony with the

54

doll's subtle coloring. This rubber doll is from the Coleman collection.

German china dolls representing children are not common, but four very fine ones have been brought together in Plate 10b to form a rare and revealing group. A comparison with plates 22 and 25a will illustrate the striking change in attitude toward children in the fifty years or so between them. There is a difference of twenty years or so between the black-haired children shown here and the blondes, and through them one can trace an increasing trend toward naturalism.

The largest and the smallest dolls of this group are the most realistic; they are also the earliest and the latest, respectively. They are very different from each other; the large doll, for all its vitality, is conceived very formally in sculptural terms whereas the little one is so photographically natural that its features are almost blurred. In character, however, they are still very much alike. These are the children who should be seen and not heard, for whose idle hands the devil could always find mischief. These dolls are from the collection of Bess Goldfinger.

There are dolls from this period with heads made from other materials—for instance, papier-mâché, and gutta-percha—which are so similar to china heads that it is almost certain that the molds in use were interchangeable. In fact, it is easy to think of these dolls as derivatives of the chinas except that there is no way of knowing which came first. Papier-mâché, as we have seen, had been used for dolls' heads since at least the beginning of the nineteenth century.

A group of such papier-mâché–headed dolls is pictured in Plate 11a, and they compare most interestingly with the chinas in plates 9 and 10b. The three lady dolls are American, made by Ludwig Greiner, of Philadelphia, under his patents of 1858 and 1872. Ludwig Greiner, an immigrant from Germany, brought with him considerable professional skill as a doll-maker. The largest doll is the earliest, and the smallest doll is the most unusual. The doll in the blue dress is in astonishingly pristine condition; she looks as if she had been made and dressed yesterday. This group demonstrates clearly the homely charm of such dolls. They were not easily broken; they were stolid and wholesome, and they must have been reassuring companions, especially to the small daughters of American pioneers.

The boy doll on the right is not a Greiner; he is of German make and is older by a quarter of a century than his companions. His head and his windblown hairstyle are vigorously modeled with considerably more plasticity than the Greiners. (The latter, which are oddly two-dimensional, remind one of those Staffordshire chimney ornaments meant to be viewed only from the front.) His glass eyes are mechanized and enable him to flirt them from side to side, a movement that gives the doll extraordinary vitality. His beautifully preserved costume is original; its smartness and dash contribute greatly to his total panache. The doll in the blue dress is from the collection of Alberta Derby; the others are from the collection of Margaret Whitton.

The outrageous dolls in Plate 11b are posed very suitably in a Victorian bathroom, for they were described by their makers as *badekinder*, or "bathing children." The examples here are remarkably large, from twelve to sixteen inches, but *badekinder* were usually trivial little dolls, costing only a penny or so. Made in one piece, without joints, they floated nicely in water. A few were made with movable limbs, however, since there were no rules about construction. The attitude of the makers of most dolls was very casual; the *badekinder*, like many other cheap, mass-produced toys, were of no great importance in their day.

Today these same toys have acquired enormous value. It is very easy for the collector who has invested a great deal of money in them to develop a false sense of proportion when reviewing his treasures. This is a pity, since it encourages an unreal appraisal of the dolls themselves. Much time can be wasted in trying to force dolls into fictitious categories created by a false sense of values while more important issues are overlooked.

The dolls in Plate 11b are startlingly large. What was charmingly trivial in the palm of the hand is suddenly a monster—heavy, unwieldy, and, one would think, very difficult for wet little hands to grasp. The girl in the foreground is an unusual exception, for most of the larger dolls are boys, and we stare at them aghast. Our picture of the prim Victorian nursery is suddenly jarred. Where are the prunes and prisms now, the chair legs carefully draped and unmentionable, the old gentlemen fainting at the glimpse of an ankle? Did fond Mama really think this great china thing a suitable and amusing toy to pop under the Christmas tree? The larger doll in particular is a very positive statement, and although he is not genitally complete, he is, with his pink face and unprotected white body, quite decidedly naked.

The dolls give one pause, and perhaps the answer is that the prunes-and-prisms prudery, pervasive as it was, was invented for and assumed by young ladies of standing, who had to be sent to the altar in a state of chaste ignorance if they were to make good marriages. In fact, if one delves into the Victorian scene, there was a good deal of nudity present, including the lauded works of art at the academies, the ornaments in the parlor, and the china fairings on the cottage shelf. We find a link between the dolls and these fairings, as recent research has disclosed that at least one factory in Germany which made these racy "jokes in porcelain" made a variety of other china objects, including dolls. Mary Hillier, in her book *Dolls and Dollmakers,** refers to a trade advertisement for such a firm, Conte and Boehme, of Saxony, which specifically lists *badekinder* among its products.

This brings us back to Plate 11b and to the dolls themselves. In a sense, they are very satisfying objects; their forms are simple and geometrical, and the concept is as three-dimensional as African sculpture. This is partly due to the technical processes involved in making such large hollow figures in ceramic. The limbs and trunk were molded separately and were assembled while the clay was soft; hence the joins are often conspicuous. Perhaps it is this system of "building" the dolls which gives them their odd, archaic look and their solid architectural weight. The ponderous sensuality of their massive limbs and gross bellies is disturbing, however, and it is difficult to reconcile these *badekinder* with one's mental picture of the Victorian nursery. The large doll in the center belongs to the author; the rest are from the collection of Kit Robbins.

* New York: G. P. Putnam's Sons, 1968.

"The Ernest Fiedler Family," painted by Heinrich in 1850. The aim is ambitious, and the parlor has been arranged to look as much like one in a great house as is possible, but the family is a cosy group amid all this grandeur, and the well-behaved children are very like the dolls we are sure they possessed. (*Museum of the City of New York*)

A large and handsome china head, of exceptionally fine quality, c. 1845 (*McDonald Archive, Museum of the City of New York*)

Two china dolls of very different character, each with inset glass eyes
(McDonald Archive, Museum of the City of New York)

Lithograph of a toy-shop window at Broadway and Canal Street, New York City, Christmas, 1865 (*Museum of the City of New York*)

A child of the 1860's, clasping her china doll. It could very well have been bought for her at the toy shop in the lithograph shown above. (*Author's Collection*)

60

A German china doll of exceptional quality, with pierced ears, c. 1870
(McDonald Archive, Museum of the City of New York)

A china boy of the late 1870's. His linen is fine and very interesting. (*Kit Robbins Collection*)

"Reading the News," from a card for the stereopticon of the late 1860's. Although this scene is contrived, it does show us a group of real little girls playing with dolls. (*Author's Collection*)

"The House That Jack Built," an elaborate set piece in Mr. Potter's Museum of Humerous Taxidermy, in Bramber, Sussex. This charming group is interesting as it not only presents us with a countryman's view of the idyllic Sussex life but also preserves for us the dolls, untouched since Mr. Potter set them in place in the 1870's. (Bramber Museum, Sussex, England)

A charming pair of *badekinder*, 2¾ inches high, dressed very completely in colored silks *(Kit Robbins Collection)*

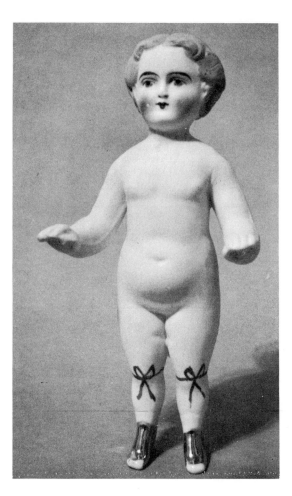

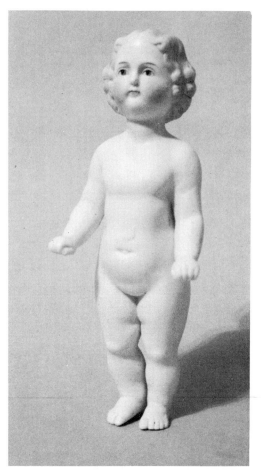

A group of three *badekinder* that gives some idea of the immense variety that was made *(Kit Robbins Collection)*

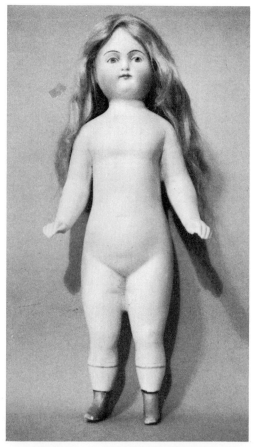

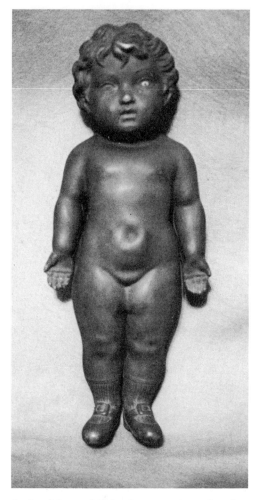

A bathing child of tan-colored rubber, made in Germany (*Kit Robbins Collection*)

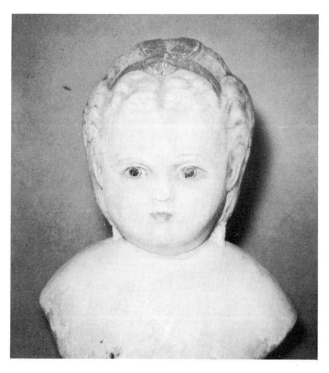

A doll's head made of hard rubber, with colored features and hair ribbon on a white ground. Unmarked, from the 1870's, this rare doll is sadly battered; originally she must have been very lovely and distinctive. (*Author's Collection*)

CHAPTER 6

Love in

Wax

In Chapter 1 we glanced at the fine wax dolls that survive from the eighteenth century and observed that these dolls were a sideline of wax-workers, whose major output was of other items. Progressing into the nineteenth century, we find wax-workers feeling the pinch for a while and then enjoying a wave of prosperity as decorative objects made of wax become increasingly fashionable during the middle of the century. Groups of figures, miniature scenes in cases, and baskets of luscious fruit or delicate flowers were made professionally in large quantities. These good times, alas, were to be short. Soon a good deal of the trade was destroyed by amateur competition as wax-working became a popular parlor employment.

There were, of course, steady requests for wax wreaths for graves, and in Catholic countries there was still a demand for religious work. It is not too outrageous to assume, however, that the vast variety of wax dolls which appeared from the 1850's onward was directly related to the lack of demand for other wax artifacts and to the needs of the workers for other sources of income.

Wax seems an unlikely and impractical material to choose for doll-making, although the results are often very pretty. There is a factor of impermanence involved here, and it is significant to note that dolls made of durable materials, such as wood, composition, and papier-mâché, were now fairly cheap; the expensive and fashionable dolls were fragile—top-heavy china, thin, brittle bisque, and friable wax.

Wax is essentially an organic material, and it has its own aesthetic qualities. It is exceptionally plastic, with a large range of surface tension. It is capable of imitating widely different textures, especially organic ones: Rough-pored leaves, smooth, shining fruit, a child's velvety skin—all can be simulated so as to deceive the eye.

Wax dolls can be divided easily into two main categories, which are quite different in origin and effect. The first division should properly be described as waxed dolls, since they are in fact composition or papier-mâché dolls that have been waxed to give them a richer finish. This is in contrast with the second group, in which the wax, the basic material, is poured or molded.

Waxed dolls make an early enough appearance (early nineteenth century) to have been among the first new ideas of the expanded German toy industry. They derive from toy-makers' crafts rather than from the ancient art of wax-working. In fact, they have a good deal in common with the old German wooden toys; their heads are modeled simply, with jovial, toy-like faces. There is very little to distinguish one doll from another.

The charming baby doll in Plate 12a is one of those made in the manner patented by Motschmann, of Sonneberg, in 1857, inspired in its turn by a doll of traditional Japanese design. In this case, the wax is merely a finishing touch to a composition head, and many of these Motschmann dolls are found without it. The composition body has turned wooden limbs with articulated floating joints; the head contains a curious joint, which was made with a system of interior tapes. A cloth

68

midsection in the torso allows a squeaker to be accommodated. The design adheres closely to the Japanese original, even to the stylized wisps of hair over the ears. Oriental dolls continued to be made, perhaps with some improvements adopted from the Germans, and because of this, it is often difficult to decide the origin of a particular doll.

Our baby here, however, is almost certainly German. His features are still brightly colored, and he still has his waxen bloom—he was probably played with very little. One suspects that the discolorations of his arms are due to climatic changes rather than to wear.

His great charm is his costume, which is intact and pristine and, we may note with interest, commercially made. Here, for once, we can hold in our hands the flimsy confectionery of net and glacé ribbon, still as delectable as it looks in paintings and fashion plates. This is the temporary prettiness, as fleeting as the freshness of cut flowers, of which we so often read: ". . . to church in the heat, my old leghorn newly trimmed with rosebuds and a good, blue feather . . ." and "We spent the rest of the day mending our tarlatans, and planning their refurbishment."

The faded sepia photographs of the period can look so dowdy, and the bright chromos are as unconvincing as the darling children on the valentines who clutch their crisp, beribboned dolls. But here is one of those dolls, still crisp, and as pretty and absurd as one could wish. His toy is also from Sonneberg, where these charming "baa-lambs" are made to this day, although the rams of the species, with their beautiful gilt horns, seem now to be extinct. The baby doll is from the Museum of the City of New York; his "baa-lamb" from the author's collection.

The boy doll in Plate 12b is from the second half of the nineteenth century and shows how beautiful this kind of waxed–papier-mâché doll can be at its best. He was conceived with great seriousness, and his face and hair are carefully detailed. This is a real little boy, not a stylized mask, and despite his infant chubbiness, he is sober and responsible. The forms of his head are sculptural and precise, the planes merging from one to another, with nothing blurred or avoided. He wears neat Sunday clothes, his blue coat matching his painted shoes. His necklaces of childishly strung beads are still around his neck, thanks to the sensitivity of his present owners.

There has always been conjecture about dolls preserved in such glass-fronted boxes, one noticeable fact being that the dolls are nearly always waxed ones. The purpose, in this instance at least, is clear, since the doll's owners have found identical cases, all containing dolls, banked inside a church in Germany. There is little doubt that this case is a similar religious offering, made probably for a dead child. In this context the little strings of beads become pathetic and moving. The doll is from the Coleman collection.

The poured-wax doll in Plate 13 is entirely different, both in concept and in effect. Eclipsed for a while at the turn of the century by the flood of commercial dolls, the beautiful products of the wax-workers largely vanished from the market, and it was a long time before they reappeared. It is not until the 1850's that we find ambitious new wax dolls, larger and more beautiful than any before, being manufactured in quantity. Plate 13 shows an example of such a doll.

By some miracle this lovely little girl has come down to us in perfect condition, the bloom of her wax undisturbed, her hair still as neatly arranged as it was before she was sold. Here we can see for ourselves not only how beautiful such dolls could be but also how very human and lovable. The thick wax here is creamy pink, flushed, and warm-looking; the flesh is plump and dimpled, and the rather voluptuous features are exquisitely modeled. The hair, brows, and lashes are set in skillfully so that they seem to grow in an entirely natural manner.

The colors of the doll and her clothing are subtly complementary. An imposing air of consequence is achieved by the assembling of rich textures—the velvety wax, spun-sugar hair, gleaming satin, and cobwebby tulle. This doll demonstrates the skills of the wax-worker at a very high level of accomplishment. She is in every way a masterpiece. This doll is from the collection of Margaret Whitton.

Two later, cheaper poured-wax dolls are shown in Plate

14a. They show by contrast a clear picture of the decline of this type of doll. The concept here is weak and imperfect. The faces, although pretty enough, are amorphous and without character. They look like little ghosts beside the brilliantly realized "person" in Plate 13. Nevertheless, they have a great deal of charm in their own right.

The wax here, although thick in substance, is thin and translucent in texture. The hair in each case is a wig, with a fringe of curls set in around the hairline. The painting of the features is identical; although the dolls were found on different continents, they seem to have come from the same factory.

The clothing in each case is handmade and has an endearing, bundly look. The colors are similar to those of the doll in Plate 13, but here the effect is very different. The tawdry little brooch—painted tin forget-me-nots—strikes exactly the right note, as does the naïve homemade paper dollhouse in the background. The doll on the left is from the author's collection. The one on the right is from the Museum of the City of New York.

Since the waxed dolls relate so closely to composition and papier-mâché ones, it seems appropriate to include a composition doll here, and in Plate 14b we have a remarkable example of this type. This doll is a commercial product of the last quarter of the nineteenth century, put away untouched, just as she came from the shop. She is extravagantly dressed and was very probably someone's "best" doll, to be looked at and gloated over but never touched.

The modeling and the color are very reminiscent of the later waxed dolls, and it is easy to transform her in our minds, imagining the color glowing through the soft, vulnerable surface. The lamb's-wool wig was once very curly, and it makes a lively contrast to her smooth cheeks.

Her clothing is most interesting, commercially made, and almost certainly sold with the doll. Yet it is so finely made and so richly ornamented that to an unpracticed eye it could pass as baby clothes made for a special occasion. Indeed, it was described by the donor as a christening dress. It is in fact a robe de chambre of the late 1870's, a garment for a lady to wear in her boudoir while resting from tight-laced corsets

71

during the endless process of changing clothes. A flat panel with princess lines runs down the front to the floor, richly ornamented with tucks and insertions. The saque back extends to form a long train, and the shoulder knots have long streamers pendent from them. The matching cap has lace lappets and is trimmed with similar ribbons. The robe is an expensive garment and a costly one to maintain; it speaks very clearly of the wealth and ease of its wearer. This elegant doll is from the Museum of the City of New York.

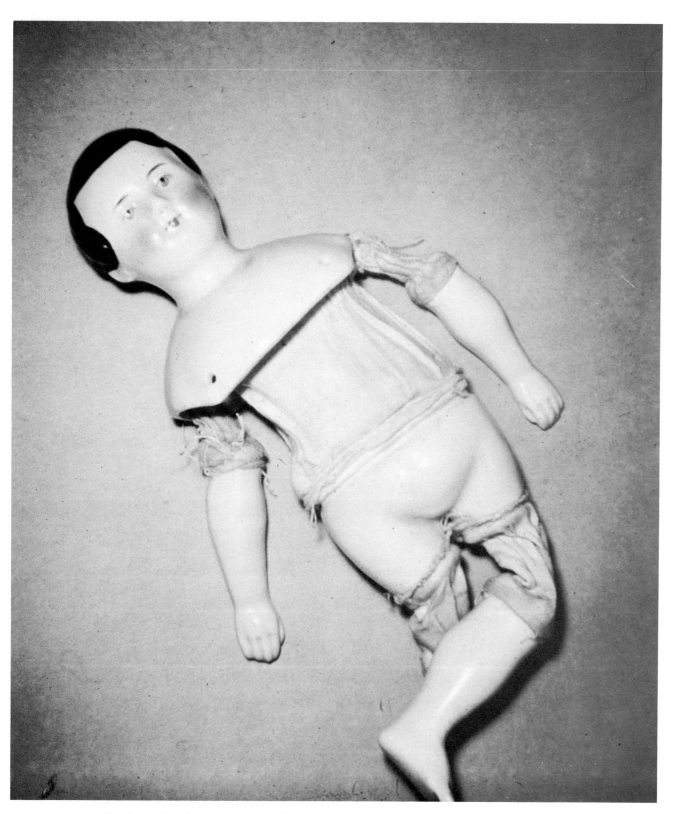

Doll with china and cloth parts similar to the doll patented by Motschmann in 1857 *(Museum of the City of New York)*

"The Wilson Children," artist unknown, c. 1860. A delightful if somewhat unlikely idyll of childhood, set in a bosky glen. Similar clothes are often found on the wax dolls of the period. (*Museum of the City of New York*)

A waxed–papier-mâché doll, beautifully preserved (*Kit Robbins Collection*)

"Rough and the Doll," from *The Prize* magazine for February, 1886. The doll is—or was—a wax one; her dress is very similar to that of her mistress. (*Author's Collection*)

A German figurine of a shepherdess standing on a mossy bank, all made of wax, c. 1850. The head is exactly in the manner of the little dressed wax dolls common at the time. Wax-workers obviously made several different kinds of objects at the same time. (*Museum of the City of New York*)

A small wax doll, c. 1850, wearing the kind of commercial dress found on examples of this type. All is very delicate and exquisite. The doll is similar but not identical to the wax shepherdess shown on the left. (*Museum of the City of New York*)

An American trade card of the late 1870's, showing little girls playing
with their wax dolls, apparently oblivious of their noisy brothers (*Kit
Robbins Collection*)

This waxed composition head was by no means expensive, but it has
very pleasant modeling, a carefully detailed wig, and brilliant, flower-
like coloring. (*Kit Robbins Collection*)

An English family photograph, in which a child stands in the parlor window, clasping her wax doll. It is Sunday—or a birthday—and the girl's best velvet dress is protected by a lacy pinafore. Perhaps the beautiful poured-wax doll is her best, too? (*Author's Collection*)

A poured-wax doll of the 1880's, dressed as a bride. Creative disproportion is at work: The doll is top-heavy, producing the quaint effect we are used to, for instance, in the drawings of Grace Drayton or Mabel Lucy Attwell. The doll and her dress are faded and crumbling, adding romance to absurdity. (*Author's Collection*)

The wax doll that this English toddler is clutching is more likely her favorite than her best one. The doll's hair, although wildly disarranged, suggests the 1870's, whereas the child's dress is from about 1885.

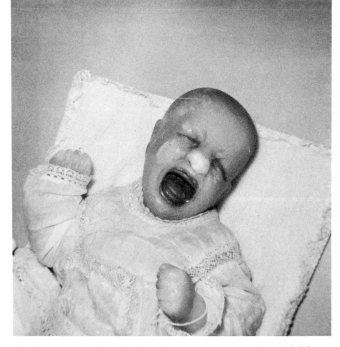

This screaming baby is disconcertingly lifelike. The poured wax of the head is extremely thick; the body is a stick. (*Kit Robbins Collection*)

Poured-wax doll of a kind that became popular in the late 1880's (*Kit Robbins Collection*)

Christmas candy box in the shape of a doll. Much of its charm lies in the contrast between the pretty wax face and the fur and hair. (*Author's Collection*)

"Pleasing decay" is an architectural term used to describe a building that is weathered but not yet in ruins. It implies that the mellowing and moldering processes that are due to exposure to the elements result in a natural state, with aesthetic qualities that are valid and acceptable. This attitude holds for other antiquities—no one today would attempt to replace the shattered limbs and noses of Greek marbles; to polish the bronze of an eroded Han Dynasty mirror would be unthinkable. The waxed dolls shown here are, in my opinion, in a state of pleasing decay. Although decrepit, they are nonetheless complete and very vital, with a great deal of their original charm still appreciable. These dolls continue to have considerable intrinsic value; to restore would be to destroy. (E. J. Carter and Coleman Collections)

CHAPTER 7

Oriental Attitudes

The two little wax dolls in Plate 15a represent Chinese children, although they were both made in Germany in the mid-nineteenth century. Like the other toys and the "Pillement" paper in the picture, they are not truly Chinese at all; they are chinoiserie creatures and belong in spirit to a decorative conceit of the previous century.

Travel to the Orient had always been difficult and dangerous, and once he arrived there, the European voyager found himself severely restricted in his movements, especially in China. Thus even eyewitnesses could tell only about tantalizing glimpses of the wondrous *pays du porcelain*. To quote Frank Davis: "What Europe built up from traveller's tales . . . was not a clear picture of a distant land and people, but a vision of Cathay as vague as that imagined by Coleridge a century and a half later, where everything was quaintly charming, and men were wise and decorative."[*]

From this vision evolved a style of decoration now known as chinoiserie, based lightheartedly, even frivolously, on Chinese

[*] "Chinoiserie Indoors," in J. Hadfield, ed., *The Saturday Book* (Boston: Little, Brown & Co., 1967), p. 87.

83

motifs, without any attempt at understanding the underlying principles that govern Chinese art. The Europeans were celebrating a fairy-tale world of Oriental fancy rather than the Orient itself.

Our two wax dolls are among the last expressions of that eighteenth-century chinoiserie, which still lingered in social backwaters. In the kitchen it decorated grocers' calendars and biscuit tins, at the theater it lent magic to the pantomime *Aladdin,* and its dreamy wonderland was very suitable for the nursery.

The doll in the red costume was made in the style of the Motschmann patent except that here, uniquely, the doll is Oriental. The features are piquant and pointed, but despite the mysterious slanted eyes and brows, the face manages still to be sweetly childlike and lovable. The waxed–papier-mâché head is tinted the same olive-yellow color as the body. The odd little coolie hat of netted silk seems to be part of the original factory-made costume—one longs for the rest. The doll has been appropriately redressed, using brocaded silk. This doll is from the collection of the Museum of the City of New York.

The doll in blue also wears a homemade dress, but this is original and seems to have been sewn by a child. It is interesting to see how the simple frock with gathered neck, straight sleeves, and pantaloons—the basic costume for thousands of wax dolls—has here been made exotic by the use of rich materials and lavish trimming. This is an Oriental version of a common, inexpensive type of wax doll. The head is made of papier-mâché, thickly waxed, a round hole accommodating the pigtail. The stuffed body is made of coarse pink cotton; the limbs are merely waxed plaster. It is easy to visualize the other little dolls, of which this is such an unusual variant. The simple black glass eyes are set in deeply slanted sockets, giving an inscrutable look that is both absurd and delightful on the chubby face.

The little doll dangling by his arm is part of a mechanical toy and is also an excellent example of tea-merchants' chinoiserie. The ridiculous cups and saucers are from a German toy tea-set, adapted almost directly from eighteenth-century porcelain. This last doll and the doll in blue are from the author's collection; the tea things are from the Museum of the City of New York.

The photographer's setting evokes exactly the dreamy, glittering wonderland, and it is remarkable that he has caught the slight nuance of outlandishness and cruelty which is a characteristic of chinoiserie on this "popular" level. One finds it even in such innocuous fantasies as *The Mikado*, of Gilbert and Sullivan, or Hans Christian Andersen's *The Emperor and the Nightingale*, two quite different visions of Cathay, in either of which our delightful dolls would be quite at home.

The Anglo-Chinese Wars, or Opium Wars, as the Chinese called them, had already shattered the illusion by the time these dolls were made. China was open to the West, and travelers to that antique land found, as Robert Fortune expressed it in words ringing with disappointment, that "the curtain which has been drawn around the celestial country for ages has now been rent asunder, and, instead of viewing an enchanted wonderland, we find after all, that China is just like other countries."*

The child doll in Plate 15b was made during the first two decades of the twentieth century and is as different as possible from the dolls we have been discussing. Here is the mental approach of the new age, with its readiness for change and expansion and its eagerness for knowledge. The magic lantern and *Grimms' Fairy Tales* had been replaced by the cinematograph and the *Children's Encyclopedia*.

This doll is a German bisque, with a typical strung composition body. It represents a toddler and is whimsically dressed in the costume of a Chinese temple-dancer. This slightly coy notion is the only fanciful thing about this doll; the head is modeled after a real Chinese baby, and the dancer's costume is remarkably accurate. This charming doll is from the collection of Dorothy Blankley. Nothing could emphasize more strongly the change that fifty years can bring to a domestic climate than the contrasts between the doll in this picture and those in the preceding one.

* Robert Fortune, quoted in Raymond Fitzsimons, "An Artist in Cathay," *ibid.*, p. 44.

Two engravings from a most interesting series published in London in 1812. Presumably illustrations for a book about life in China, they depict vendors of toys, with children playing beside them. The "vision of Cathay" has faded here, and the figures are only one step removed from English countryfolk. (*Kit Robbins Collection*)

Rockingham porcelain figure of a woman in pseudo-Chinese dress, c. 1830. The waist of the "Oriental" robe has been tightened, the collar pulled open, and the sleeves exaggerated to suggest the silhouette of contemporary fashionable dress. (*Victoria and Albert Museum, London*)

"Tea and Coffee," a plate from *Les Fleurs animées* by J. J. Grandville, published in Paris in 1847. The lady who represents tea is wearing a sketchy version of Chinese dress, but very little attempt has been made at accuracy. The highly improbable tripod table is meant to be Chinese too. Here is a make-believe world in which the dolls of Plate 15a would have felt very much at home. (*Kit Robbins Collection*)

A mechanical Chinaman doll with a waxed head and hat, c. 1870 (*Dorothy Blankley Collection*)

Four beautiful Oriental bisques, made between 1900 and 1920 in Germany. Like the child in Plate 15b these are serious, dignified ethnic conceptions of surprising accuracy. (*Dorothy Blankley Collection*)

CHAPTER 8

Ringlets and Ribbons

Here is a most enchanting category of dolls which, alas, has suffered more than most from the debasement and distortion of uninformed hearsay. This is a great pity, since the spirit of these dolls is fragile and easily blurred, but perceived with a clear vision, it has a lyrical freshness not often matched.

The late 1860's and 1870's saw the blossoming of a taste for prettiness and extravagance and an enthusiasm for youth and sunshine after the brooding restraints of previous decades. There were many causes for this change of outlook: Greater economic security was one, and the rapid increase in personal comfort, which went hand in hand with invention and discovery, was another. As industry became increasingly mechanized, prosperity spread and ideas burgeoned. One gets the feeling that in the 1870's, for the first time in several decades, young people felt that they were living in a golden age.

The dolls we are considering here, which are called fancy bisques in contemporary writings, are a reflection of this mood. They are directly related to the fashions in decorated chinaware (manufacturers of the chinaware obviously made the dolls as a sideline), and it is not difficult to locate figurines with heads that show distinct family resemblances. The individual manufacturers of these dolls are as yet unknown, although it is possible to recognize several distinctive types.

There was a new rage for elaborately decorated figurines, lamps, candlesticks, and vases, festooned with applied ribbons, and garlands of leaves and flowers. They echo the bocage* of the fine porcelain of a century earlier but with a very different effect. By this time John Ruskin and the Pre-Raphaelites had pointed out that Art was the servant of Nature.

Very few of these ornaments of the 1870's can be rated among the finest achievements of the potter's art. Too often they are weakly conceived, the forms derivative and flaccid, with nothing of the clarity and conviction of their eighteenth-century prototypes or the vitality of some of the radical developments that were to follow.

Curiously enough, when the style is transferred from the figurine to the doll, the aesthetic standard changes. When the decorated head is detached from the static ornament and incorporated with leather and other fabrics to form a doll, it at once gains in richness and vitality. In addition, the doll has a far more complex function; it is made to be handled and played with. It possesses the extra dimension of motion, which the figurine does not have. On the figurine the head is a fixed focal point; on the doll it is a contributing element in an assembly of variables. The doll has also considerably more potential emotionally, and this factor adds to its liveliness. The force of these arguments can be simply demonstrated by taking the heads from several such dolls and setting them in a china cabinet in the company of similar figurines and vases. Much of their vitality and power will immediately disappear.

So far, no very clear picture has been given of these dolls, other than that they are decorated. Several beautiful examples will be found in Plate 16a. As usual, the earlier dolls are aesthetically the better ones. The china seems to be of finer

---

* A term, used in the field of ceramics, which refers to leafy, flowery backgrounds sometimes found on china figurines of the eighteenth and nineteenth centuries.

Plate 9. German china dolls, c. 1850–1860

Plate 10a.
Rubber doll, c. 1870

Plate 10b.
German china children,
c. 1860–1885

Plate 11a.
German and American
papier-mâché dolls, c. 1845–1870

Plate 11b. German *badekinder,*
or bathing dolls, c. 1860

93

Plate 12a. German wax baby, Motschmann type, c. 1855

Plate 12b. "Charles," a German waxed–papier-mâché doll, c. 1865

Plate 13. English (?) poured-wax doll, c. 1870

Plate 14a.
English (?) poured-wax dolls,
c. 1885–1890

Plate 14b.
German composition doll, c. 1875

Plate 15a. German wax dolls,
representing Orientals,
c. 1860–1880

Plate 15b.
German bisque-headed baby doll,
dressed as a Chinese temple-dancer,
c. 1910

97

Plate 16a.
German bisque dolls,
c. 1865–1875

Plate 16b. German bisque dolls,
called hooded chinas or fancies,
c. 1890–1900

quality, and the workmanship is painstaking. The three dolls presented here are imaginative, and captivating.

The largest was made in the mid-1860's. The head is not decorated except for the molded necklace, and the hair is arranged very simply. The modeling of the face is full of character and is carefully observed. The smallest doll was made ten years later, and the features are a little more stereotyped; the artist seems to have been primarily interested in realizing the intricacies of braids and curls and in contrasting glossy ribbon with demure frills. The doll on the right, again from the mid-1860's, is entirely different in concept. Her round little face is exaggeratedly prim, the features bunched together, with popping eyes and a pursed rosebud mouth. In the face of the largest doll the forms are assembled three-dimensionally, as they would be in sculpture, but in this face there is almost no form, the features being depicted on a flat surface in a curiously primitive manner. These dolls are from the collection of Margaret Whitton.

The enviable group of a dozen rare fancy-bisque heads in Plate 17 is the property of the Museum of the City of New York, which is fortunate to own no less than twenty-eight of these beautiful heads. A family resemblance is noticeable among these ladies, and several of them are marked with similar sequences of figures and letters—presumably a code system to identify the molds.

Most of the ladies have a startling look of awareness, whether their eyes are painted or inset glass. Their faces have a wash of pale-pink skin-color, their blond hair is arranged elaborately, and the jewels, ribbons, and flowers which decorate their hair are often glazed and heightened with gilding. Some have pierced ears, although many of the earrings are now missing.

The two heads in the center row are part of a series of dolls wearing peasant headdresses; it would be exciting to locate some of the others. The lady from the Near East has black hair, which is extremely rare among these dolls. A long gold tassel hangs from the back of her cap. The Italian lady's folded linen headdress is carefully delineated, as are the details of her blouse.

Perhaps the rarest of these heads are the two children, the fat baby in her frilly bonnet and the boy in the forage cap. They are certainly the most endearing. This group is in the Museum of the City of New York.

It would be fascinating to trace the progress of the dolls of this type from the peak of their success through the various stages of decline during the next few decades. As this is not possible here, I have chosen to pinpoint one of those later stages—one that became enormously popular during the late 1890's.

These dolls were known in contemporary print as hooded chinas or fancies. One series that wore flowers or insects as headgear were described as Marguerite dolls. A group of sixteen dolls of this type are displayed in Plate 16b.

They are, of course, the descendants of the above-mentioned fancy-bisque dolls, but they are very different indeed from their antecedents. For one thing, they are a much poorer product, for the bisque itself is coarse and heavy. They have more in common with the dolls made of candy that used to be sold at Christmas time. They have the same sugariness and, for all their slapdash bravura, a transitory look, as though they were not meant to last.

They were very cheap, and one has the feeling that they were never very important, either to their makers or to the children who received them. They must have been very popular, however, considering the enormous variety that was made. They cannot have been produced over a very long period—ten to fifteen years at the most—and yet there are literally dozens of different heads, all produced in several sizes. A grouping such as this emphasizes their brittle gaiety, which must have been familiar to most little girls at the end of the century.

Comparing them with the decorated heads in Plate 17 is an interesting study in the shifting of aesthetic values. The cheapening of the product, of course, presents many contributing factors—the coarseness of the bisque, the loose limpidity of the painting—but these little dolls also send back a small, clear echo of the changing taste in art.

The earlier fancy bisques, in their way, paid some homage to Ruskin and the worship of Nature as well as to the accepted standards of academic art. The "hooded chinas" make their connection with the Arts and Crafts movement and with Walter Crane. Several of the dolls in the picture are wearing the romantic hats inspired by the Stuart period, which was in high favor since it had the approval of Charles Eastlake and his admirers. The coloring of these dolls, as far as the crude pigments will allow, is consciously "artistic," and we find them wearing indigo, maroon, dull olive, and sage green, colors that would have been unthinkable to the potters of 1860. And in the Marguerite series, where tenuously modeled insects are poised on the dolls' heads, we can catch more than a hint of the influence of Art Nouveau. From the collections of Kit Robbins and the author.

In a contemporary lithograph a little girl of the late 1890's wanders through a toy store. The picture is full of information, but we notice particularly that the Oriental doll is now an authentic Japanese import, and that real Japanese lanterns decorate the store. (*Kit Robbins Collection*)

English porcelain fruit-dish, painted and gilded, made by Minton in 1853. The allegorical figures are of the Parian ware developed by Minton in the 1840's. The misuse of the word "Parian" as a name for various fancy-bisque dolls was perpetrated by collectors in the 1920's, and there is now great confusion as to its validity. In fact, the only doll that could sensibly be called Parian would be one made of Minton or Copeland Parian ware or of one of the wares that specifically imitate them; that is, it would be made of a waxy, feldspathic porcelain resembling white marble, and the only color would be a blue or green background. Such a doll has yet to be found. (*Museum of the City of New York*)

A most beautiful little bisque doll, molded in one piece, softly colored, with touches of gilt. The fanciful Italian costume is finely detailed; rose-pink streamers fly from the straw hat. There was surely a companion girl doll, and one longs to find her. (*Kit Robbins Collection*)

Twin dolls from the late 1870's. They have bisque heads with elaborately curled and chastely beribboned hair, inset glass eyes, and very unusual bodies, with spindly arms made of rawhide. They are alike enough to be confusing, except that their dresses are trimmed with silk ribbons of different colors. (*Museum of the City of New York*)

The beautiful and elaborate bisque head of this doll has a coiffure that is enameled a glossy black, whereas the red rose in the hair is left in the mat bisque, as is the molded neckline of the blouse. The effect is very rich and lively. (*McDonald Archive, Museum of the City of New York*)

A boy doll with a serious face and crisp blond
curls, made in the late 1870's (Author's Collection)

A doll made similarly to the curly-haired blond
boy doll shown above, also from the late 1870's
(McDonald Archive, Museum of the City of
New York)

A late bisque doll with molded jewelry (McDonald Archive, Museum of the City of New York)

A photograph of a lady of the 1870's, her hair in one of the elaborate styles found on the fancy-bisque dolls (Author's Collection)

One of the later bisques, with gilt-touched molded and glazed ruffles and ornaments (*McDonald Archive, Museum of the City of New York*)

Head of a German bisque figurine of the 1890's, decorated with molded flowers and painted very freely; the quality and color are very reminiscent of the so-called bonnet dolls (*Author's Collection*)

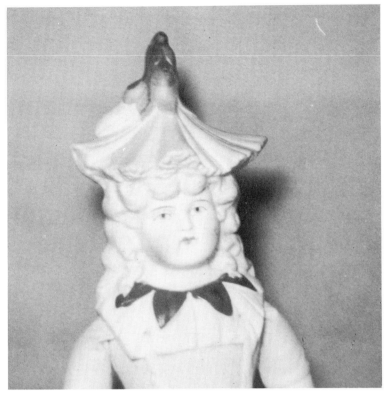

A head in coarse bisque, wearing an inverted blossom as a hat. The doll has great poise, and the color is sweet and lyrical. (*Kit Robbins Collection*)

A group of so-called Marguerite dolls that wear insects and flowers in the manner and with the lines of fashionable headgear, all molded in the bisque (*Kit Robbins Collection*)

German embossed "scraps" from the 1890's, with an obvious affinity
with the Marguerite dolls (Kit Robbins Collection)

CHAPTER 9

French Elegance

Doll-making in France is an industry that seems to have grown up very quickly during the 1850's. There were, of course, dolls made before this date but not on any important scale.

The sudden rise of this major industry was perhaps not unrelated to the efforts of the Empress Eugénie to encourage the luxury trades of her country. It is known that she deliberately launched many of the extravagant styles of the midcentury—including the ever-swelling crinolines, exotic fabrics, and new, expensive colors—not for personal aggrandizement, as her predecessors had done, but in an attempt to reestablish the French silk industry and to create a world market for its products. Even today a French label implies elegance and refinement. From the first, the French china dolls were the epitome of this elegance.

The dolls seem to have sprung into existence with remarkable speed and with apparently no background in such doll-making behind them. Suddenly there were dolls on the market which were unlike any that had existed before, their structure a synthesis of the skills employed in many of the decorative

111

arts for which France was famous. The potter, the joiner, the wigmaker, the tailor, and above all the dressmaker were important contributing craftsmen. One feels that surely there must have been primary experimental stages, in which the dolls were simple if not crude. If such dolls existed, however, there were either so few that they have disappeared, or else they are so dissimilar that they survive unrecognized.

Most of the earliest examples have glazed china heads. They are poised and cool, and they seem well aware of their excellence. They display from the outset a variety of materials, and the ingenuity of their construction suggests eager, imaginative experiment. Once started, the French doll-makers seem to have worked in a frenzy of enthusiasm as one exquisite model after another left their hands. Their dolls became increasingly lavish in concept and unstinting in their consumption of labor. They were always expensive—sometimes fantastically so—and they were aimed at the newly prosperous middle classes everywhere.

The repressive figure of Queen Victoria has given a misleading aura to at least one half of the nineteenth century. By 1860 the general picture was by no means demure, and the zest for display and conspicuous consumption affected everyone. The aristocracy still lived in unfettered ease in every country, and the middle classes aped them to the fullest extent of their pockets. Below the subtle but decisive line that removed the gentry from the rest, no one was so poor that he could not make some attempt to "cut a dash." In the slums of London to this day, this impulse is still very strong. The meanest streets display fine curtains and fresh flowers in brightly polished windows, belying the poverty and hardship in the rooms behind, and it is a poor-spirited factory girl who cannot appear on Sunday dressed to kill.

This mania for display accelerated through the 1870's and 1880's, embracing the spectrum of the family, including the children. For every little girl at this time, the possession of a fine French doll represented the height of luxury. Four superb examples of these earlier dolls are to be found in plates 18a and 18b.

The doll in the blue dress in Plate 18a has the mark of Mlle. Marie Antoinette Léontine Rohmer stamped across her bosom. Mlle. Rohmer is known to have been making dolls as early as 1857, when she was granted patents for her dolls' bodies. This doll has a wooden body, covered with kid and precisely jointed. Her lower limbs, head, and shoulder plate are made of glazed china. The neck has a flat so-called cup-and-saucer joint often found on Rohmer dolls. The face is alert and distinctive; its modeling is very subtle, as is that of the hands and feet. The doll in the striped dress is unmarked, but she closely resembles the first doll except that she is not glazed and her body, including the legs and feet, is made of stitched, stuffed kid.

None of the clothing is original. The striped dress, which is marked "Huret, Paris," belongs to the larger doll in Plate 18b, as do the hats and accessories. The blue dress is an original dress of the period but was not made for this doll. Both dolls are from the Museum of the City of New York.

The two dolls in Plate 18b are unmarked. They are of a type that is associated with Maison Huret, which is known to have been making dolls in Paris since 1850. This possible origin for these dolls is strengthened, at least in the case of the larger doll, by the fact that she possesses a trunk with the elaborate paper label of Maison Huret. It is full of clothes and accessories, and the dresses, which all have the gilt Huret label, fit the doll perfectly.

Both dolls have stitched kid bodies with glazed china arms and shoulder heads. The modeling is light and deft, the painting exquisite. The brilliance of the glaze colors is enhanced by the inset eyes of rich-blue glass. These heads have a curiously insouciant air, reminiscent of the frivolous porcelain "toys" of the previous century.

The clothing of each of these dolls is remarkably fine. One wonders if the beautiful pink silk is from Lyons; the skirt here is mounted on a heavier lining so that the effect is bouffant. The ribbons and frills are lighthearted but not fussy. The gray dress is fine, smooth wool with a closely woven stripe. If the fabric could be identified, it would perhaps be found to have one of those charming and characteristic names like bombazine, jaconet, grenadine. The pink shawl is a woolen web so fine that it will drift in the air. The identical straw hats are trimmed in the fashionable manner with rosettes beneath the

113

brim. These dolls are from the Museum of the City of New York.

The lady in Plate 19a is a magnificent example of this luxurious French doll at the height of its success. The swiveled head, superbly modeled and colored, is mounted on an intricately jointed, carved, and painted wooden body similar to those used traditionally for artists' "lay" figures. Even the wrists, ankles, and waist are articulated so that the doll can assume the most lifelike positions.

Her dress, from the late 1870's, is a veritable tour de force. The cut and finish are as perfect as they would have been for a real dress, and the expensive silks are chosen exactly to scale. The pleating, piping, and other trimmings are all hand-stitched and perfect. Her underclothing is complete and correct, and as she turns to us in her progress, the dress follows her movements with all the authority of haute couture.

In Plate 19b three lovely dolls demonstrate the many costly techniques used in the construction of these dolls by their various makers. None of the three can be identified. The lady in the foreground has a stitched kid body but articulated wooden arms with bisque forearms. Her bisque head swivels on its shoulder plate. The modeling is quite different from that of most dolls of this kind; the painted eyes droop, and the full little mouth has a pronounced smile. The bisque is quite different too, with a thick creamy surface reminiscent of some of the German fancy bisques. Indeed, it has been suggested in some quarters that dolls of this particular type are of German origin. Very little is known about these lady dolls, and it is not unlikely that many of the parts, including the china ones, were ordered from Germany, where the industry was well established. By the 1880's very lovely lady dolls were being marketed in Germany. It is best, where so much must be conjecture, to cultivate an open mind.

On the right is another unmarked doll, with a very distinctive head and unusually deep blue glass eyes. Her wooden body is well articulated, enabling her to curtsy so gracefully. Each wooden section is neatly faced with kid, so that the joints work unhindered. Her young-girl's dress of oyster satin is from the early seventies, and it is made most professionally, its

114

complicated structure beautifully finished. Her bisque hands are unusually relaxed and natural.

The lady with the parasol is extremely rare and interesting. She is marked on her rib cage with the oval stamp of the Widow Clement, who distributed dolls in Paris in the 1870's. In 1867 a Pierre Victor Clement was issued a patent for making dolls of embossed leather, and the doll here has a very light, strong body, which is made of pressed, or molded, leather. The faille dress in pink, fawn, and bronze has been made very professionally. The flowered hat and parasol are correct and harmonious but do not belong to her. The doll curtseying in Plate 19b is from the author's collection. The others in both Plates 19a and 19b are from the Museum of the City of New York.

So far, these examples have illustrated the costly and stylish clothes that were provided for the dolls in Paris, but not all of them, apparently, were sold with these expensive outfits. Examples are often found wearing decidedly homemade garments, and whereas it could be argued that these dolls are the much-loved ones whose clothes wore out quickly, the fact that this is not always necessarily so is nicely demonstrated by the endearing bridal couple shown on page 123.

This pretty pair is fortunately documented; we know that the dolls were bought and dressed in Maine for a little girl named Mabel Gray Potter on her twelfth birthday. The dolls' given names are Ethel and Frederick. They are both French lady dolls, with bisque socket heads and stitched and stuffed kid bodies. Frederick has been made manly with a fashionably cut wig and a dashing moustache.

They must have been very expensive presents. The groom's suit, for instance, has been properly tailored, and his impeccable top hat is hand-sewn with similarly accomplished ease. The bride's clothes are sewn with neatness and skill suggestive of a hired dressmaker rather than a doting mama, but despite all this care and expense, the dolls remain disarmingly provincial, and the wedding dress, although tasteful and fashionable enough, seems nevertheless almost rustic compared with the elegant clothes from Paris. This artlessness, of course, is exactly what makes these otherwise ordinary dolls so desirable.

Not the least of their charm is the evidence of wit employed in assembling them. Two more-felicitous dolls could not have been chosen. Ethel is just the right size to appear helpless and protectable; her features are small and piquant, and one hopes that the slightly vixenish look given her by the straight brows and sharp little mouth is by choice and not by accident. In contrast, Frederick seems tall and capable, his face honest and open, with wide eyes and a very young, self-conscious moustache.

The birthday party, of course, was the bridal pair's wedding feast, and a few of the presents remain. Most brides get two of something, and Ethel received two pretty enamel watches; in fact, she had rather a lot of jewelry. The going-away dress has survived, and it was made by the same capable hands; the blue woolen cloth is a sensible choice for a cold climate. Someone very loving took the trouble to make her two fancy and much beribboned woolen garments, a shawl and a little jacket, to wear inside a chilly house; the tiny, complicated stitches of the fancy pattern are exquisite. Only one of the bridegroom's presents remains—a riding crop. Again, we wonder who had the sense of humor.

Bisque-headed doll made by Maison Huret in the 1860's. The plump, dreamy face is very typical. (*Museum of the City of New York*)

A fashion plate from *Le Moniteur de la mode* for 1856, showing children dressed similarly to the dolls in plates 18a and 18b. The costumes of the three little boys are the most remarkable element here. "Ferdinand" (third from right) has a good deal of masculine bravura, but it takes an attuned eye to distinguish "Petit Matelot" (second from left) and "Irlandaise" (extreme right) from their sisters. (*Museum of the City of New York*)

A fine French lady with bisque head and arms, most elaborately dressed
(*McDonald Archive, Museum of the City of New York*)

In these two fashion plates, each child displays a French doll that wears a costume similar to the one worn by its owner. (*Kit Robbins Collection*)

A French lady doll with bisque swiveled head and stitched kid body. Her summer dishabille for the late 1860's is simple and striking; the colors are scarlet and black, with everything finished to perfection. (*Author's Collection*)

A fashion plate of fashions for children, 1875. The dresses of the young ladies are particularly interesting, as the lady dolls were often dressed in these not-quite-adult styles. (*Author's Collection*)

A rare French lady doll made to represent a mulatto, with a beautiful dark tint to the bisque. The color of the kid body matches exactly (*Margaret Whitton Collection*)

A doll similar to the mulatto doll shown above, dressed in a fanciful Near Eastern costume (*Leona Peterson Collection*)

Fancy dress seems to have been a fashionable amusement of the 1870's, and perhaps this accounts for the number of dolls found dressed in ethnic costumes or puzzling fancy attire. Dolls can be found wearing variants of most of the costumes depicted in this plate; the Indian maiden, for instance, wears finery very similar to the Near Eastern costume worn by the doll shown at the bottom of page 121. (*Museum of the City of New York*)

"Ethel and Frederick," dolls bought for Mabel Gray Potter, of Maine, for her twelfth birthday. Ethel wears a fashionable wedding dress of about 1845. (*Author's Collection*)

CHAPTER 10

Children

of Paris

In the late 1870's a new kind of child doll appeared on the French market. It was an instant success, and there was a rush of competition. Dolls of all sizes and from many different makers burst upon the scene as though it were suddenly a children's holiday. The child dolls were called *bébés*, a significant name, since up to this time most dolls, including the popular ladies, had been known as *poupées*.

It has been suggested that the reason for their sudden appearance was the invention of a new type of doll body which occurred at this time. It consisted of a hollow trunk and ball-jointed limbs, all strung together with elastic, and supporting a bisque head that fitted into a socket. This body was certainly eminently suitable for suggesting the chubby limbs and gawky stances of childhood. All *bébés* were not made this way, however. Many of them still retained the stitched and stuffed kid bodies common to the lady dolls, and some makers, Bru Jne & Cie, for instance, seemed to delight in complicated and beautiful body constructions.

125   To find the true reasons for the sweeping popularity of

these child dolls, we must turn again to social history. Enormous changes were taking place in the structure of society everywhere, both in Europe and in America, and in many ways the end of the 1870's was a watershed. Political and moral reforms were in the air, and mechanical innovations were being made that were destined to cause abrupt and violent changes. At the beginning of the new decade we detect an air of alertness and excitement. The 1880's, like the 1800's and the 1920's, were to be "modern" times.

The nouveaux riches had quickly established themselves and become less conspicuously "nouveau," but their standards increasingly colored the mood of the period. The fashionable lady was no longer demure or downcast; her cloudy inaccessibility had been replaced by a bright parrot smartness. She was self-possessed, and her dress and home furnishings loudly proclaimed her wealth and importance as well as her growing independence.

In the previous chapter we spoke of the mania for display, for conspicuous consumption. In the 1880's this impulse was still very strong. When the lady was accompanied by her children, whether in public or while receiving at home, the children had to be as fine as possible, and if the little girl was to carry a doll, it too had to be fine. It is not surprising then that the new *bébés* were outfitted with quite preposterous richness and charm.

In Plate 20 a number of these *bébés* have been grouped to show a little of the wide variety of them available during this extravagant decade. With one exception they have the typical elastic-strung ball-jointed bodies. By chance, their costumes cover the seasons, presenting a panorama of what an elegant *bébé* might wear throughout the year. We will examine them from left to right.

The small seated doll on the left is from the famous firm of Jumeau. Her piquant little bisque face is set with enormous melting eyes and is framed with a wig of human hair, under which is the red "Tête Jumeau" stamp. Her beautiful homemade clothes have not been disturbed since she was put away in the early 1880's. Her summer dress of light damasked silk is the pale, subtle color known as duck's-egg blue in the days when such delicious farm fare was to be seen in every grocer's

126

shop. The matching bonnet has a gauze ruche of the same color, and both garments are trimmed with love knots of ivory silk ribbon. Obviously, this doll and her fragile costume have been carefully preserved.

The name of the maker of the standing doll in deeper blue is unknown, although his (or her) dolls are immediately recognizable, with their fine, petal-like bisque, their curiously heavy features, and their full, slightly goiterous throats. If the wigs are removed, the heads are found to have a pronounced flare, making the backs of the heads larger than most. The example here is unmarked. She is most unusual in that she has an open mouth, molded but not cut, with neatly modeled teeth. Her jointed ankles too are distinctive and unusual.

Her dress is a trifle too large for her; it is tailored with such skill that it would certainly have fitted its original owner perfectly, and so one must assume it was not always our doll's. Again, the dress is homemade of a fine woolen fabric, with tiny black checks on a brilliant blue ground. The pleated skirt is trimmed with elaborate dags and decorated with brass buttons. This autumn costume is completed with a little military cap of the same fabric. The lace-trimmed hat, which also belongs to the doll, was substituted in the heat of photographing as more harmonious to the picture. One regrets this decision at leisure, and in any case this is the sort of license that should not be taken.

The standing doll in the dark-red dress is also an enigma. She has a head with a closed crown, pierced with holes through which the strings of the legs are threaded, thus securing the head in position. Dolls with this type of head are known to collectors as Belton dolls, although no connection with the doll-maker of that name is established. The head here is unusual in that it has three holes instead of the usual two. It is unmarked except for the number "117."

It is the body of this doll, however, that is most extraordinary. Unnecessary details of the anatomy are modeled with remarkably inaccurate detail. Shoulder blades, muscles (in particular, recti abdominis and latissimi dorsi), accumulations of fatty tissue at wrists, hips, and stomach—all are painstakingly defined with care. It is not pretty, but we forget once the doll is dressed, for she is grace and charm personified.

Her costume is a winter dress, made of garnet-colored silk velvet, heavily lined and deeply pleated. It was made at least five years later than those of her companions. There are stockings to match and bronze kid shoes. The demure ruched bonnet and the high waist with its half sash suggest the influence of Kate Greenaway. This too is a homemade costume, complete with elaborate underclothes. The pretty pink enamel watch came with her.

In the center of the photograph is a doll made by Schmitt et Fils, of Paris, and has their mark, with its crossed hammers, incised into its neck and stamped on its body. The typical gauntlet-shaped forearms can be seen pulling at the tight sleeves. The Schmitt dolls are notable for their extremely fine quality and for a remarkable look of alertness and vivacity; this little doll is certainly no exception.

Her toilette is meant for a spring day in Paris. It is a triumph of professional dressmaking; fine shell-pink cashmere is bound with silk and lined with sateen, all tailored with microscopic perfection. The parasol is a commercial accessory, although its plum-colored brocade matches exactly the silk trimmings of the dress. The hat is a replica in old materials of the ruined original.

On the extreme right, also dressed for spring in pink cashmere, is a *bébé* by another great doll-maker, Bru Jne et Cie, which is marked "Bru Jne" on the back of the neck and on the left shoulder. She has the elaborate body often found on these dolls, the stuffed kid body with wooden lower legs and bisque lower arms. The upper sections of the limbs have very complicated tongued ball-joints that fit into metal limbs, which are closely covered with kid. This superb doll, like most Brus, has a curious and compelling aura. Restrained and elegant to the point of severity, she has at the same time a look of such childish wistfulness as to provoke an immediate pang of sympathy.

The tiny doll in the arms of the *bébé* Bru is of the same manufacture as the ones in the foreground. All are made of bisque, are jointed, have closed crowns under their wigs, and are unmarked. They have enormous brilliantly blue glass eyes and are usually assumed by collectors to be French dolls. Their commercial clothes look very Parisian, and they were to be bought in the toy shops of Paris. Many of them have been

128

found in the trunks of French *bébés,* doing duty as the dolls' dolls. There may, of course, be marked examples; the only one known to this writer is surprisingly incised "S & H"—for Simon and Halbig, a famous German factory. This German marking serves to remind us that the world of dolls was not insular. There was a busy international market, and component parts as well as completed dolls were exchanged briskly among doll-makers in different countries.

This group of *bébés* has been arranged as a child might play with them. The tea set is a classic toy, and today little girls are still happily arranging dolls' tea parties. We have tried to show something of the love and care that was lavished on these beautiful French *bébés* as well as their absurd, precocious charm. The three little dolls in the foreground are from the collection of Kit Robbins, and the rest are from the author's collection.

So far, we have seen *bébés* dressed at home, albeit with great skill and care. In Plate 21 two *bébés* Jumeau are presented as their makers envisaged them, dressed from top to toe in their original commercial costumes with plum satin Jumeau armbands proudly proclaiming their excellence in letters of gold leaf.

These dolls represent the peak of luxury: such pleats, ruchings, and flounces, so many complications of closures and fasteners, such costly and subtle colors. The fabrics are used with careless extravagance: satin and velvet, faille and brocade, taffeta, lace, and gauze—all are worn with conviction and poise. There is nothing reticent or imprecise about these fabulous little dolls. Like the ladies whose tastes and standards they reflect, they are decidedly present. The larger doll is from the collection of Maureen Popp, and the smaller one is from the collection of Margaret Whitton.

"Wedding Presents" by James Wells Champney, painted in 1880.
Besides giving us a glimpse of fashionable summer costume, this picture
is a fascinating reflection of the taste of the 1880's; the gifts on the
table were presumably highly desirable. The bride is suitably pensive.
Notice her grandmother's hairstyle, which is in the fashion of the 1830's
and is now fifty years out of date. (*Museum of the City of New York*)

130

A *bébé* Bru, with typical lamb's-wool wig, in a late 1870's costume.
(McDonald Archive, Museum of the City of New York)

131

Fashion plate from *Le Journal des enfants* for September, 1884, depicting a group of the sophisticated, elegant Parisian children who are reflected in the *bébés*. Their own *bébé* has a most handsome cradle. (*Author's Collection*)

A French fashion plate of 1880. An elegant little girl is being offered a kid-bodied *bébé* from a stall in a Parisian arcade. The doll is even more splendidly dressed than the child herself (*Kit Robbins Collection*)

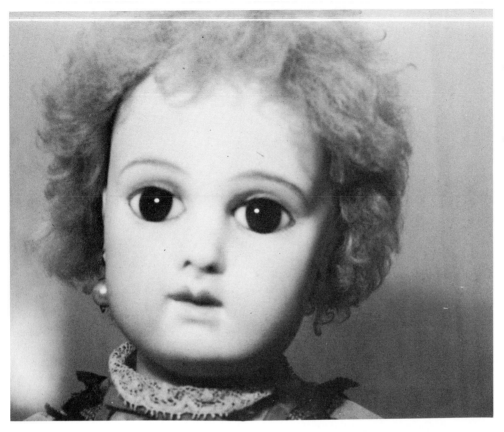

A *bébé* with an unmarked head of melting beauty. The body is marked "Jumeau, Medaille d'Or." (*Kit Robbins Collection*)

This sturdy boy doll and his sisters are from the same maker. They are marked only "Breveté" ("patented"). The twins are a rare small size. One has blue eyes, the other has brown. (*Museum of the City of New York*)

In this enchanting plate we see clearly how important style and fashion were to the Parisians of the 1880's. It would be difficult to invent more unsuitable clothes for children to wear when playing by the sea. (Author's Collection)

"Cornelia Ward Hall and Her Children," painted c. 1880 by Michael Gordigiani, shows the luxury and ease of Paris, transported to New York. The most lavish French *bébé* would not intimidate these little girls. (*Museum of the City of New York*)

A *bébé* Jumeau, dressed in its original costume as an Arab, with remarkably authentic fabrics and colors. The applied beard is beautifully shaped. Unfortunately, such ethnic costumes, so popular at the time, appealed not at all to the tastes of the early collectors, and many of the outfits have been replaced by optimistic restorations of little girls' clothes. In this way our concept of these French dolls has been altered and devitalized. (*Sylvia Brockman Collection*)

CHAPTER 11

German Inventions

The French lady and child dolls are unlike any of those examined earlier, and it would be very easy to assume that all the unmarked dolls made in this manner must of necessity be French. This is by no means the case. The toy trade was a very competitive international market. There were many early instances of copying and pirating; it was very unlikely that the French would be allowed to keep the beautiful dolls that they had invented to themselves. We know that some of the component parts of French dolls were ordered from Germany, and it is perfectly feasible that some of the lovely bisque heads were also commissioned from German factories. There are a number of marked dolls, some of them surprisingly early, to prove this point.

The beautiful doll shown on page 144 illlustrates how foolish it is to close the mind to the complexities of the doll world. It would be easy to say that this is a French doll, and a very fine one. She has many of the characteristics—such as the lady-like proportions, the beautifully finished clothes, the enormous melting eyes, and above all, the remarkably fine shoulder head and forearms of delicately and sensitively modeled bisque, pale and subtle in color—that we associate with the French dolls.

This typically French head, however, is clearly marked by Simon and Halbig, the porcelain factory of Thüringen, Germany, famous for its many beautiful dolls' heads. The doll's cloth body bears the stamp of R. Eekhoff, of Groningen, in the Netherlands, who appears in Leuch's trade directory under "Toys" in 1894. The stamp is not dated, and, of course, the doll could have been made a good deal earlier than the entry in the directory. The costume is that of a peasant of the Groningen province, the metal helmet signifying that she is married. The clothes are seriously and accurately made, and they add considerably to the interest and value of this unusual doll.

Popular taste at the turn of the century was heavily inclined toward the photographic and the literal, and it is not surprising that the German doll-makers, as their bisque dolls gained favor, should press their advantage by attempting to improve their wares with all kinds of lifelike details: eyes with multiple movements, inset eyelashes and inlaid eyebrows made of fur, tongues that could move and tremble, and so on. Naturalism was achieved in other directions, by giving the dolls definite characters and expressions. These dolls contrast greatly with the cheaper dolls, whose prettiness seems insipid and whose smiles are vacant in comparison.

Such a striking contrast can be found in the doll shown on page 145. This ball-jointed, bisque-headed example represents a grown woman, and she is very different from any of the dolls we have examined. This lady is lifelike in a completely photographic manner, the features irregular and impressionistic, the expression most enigmatic and undoll-like. This too is a Simon and Halbig head, but it is very different from that of the Dutch peasant lady we were discussing. The costume, which is from about 1910, is artistically muted in color and made of delicate chiffon and charmeuse silk.

She was very difficult to arrange for photographing. The glade of fresh, pale irises we had intended for her could not be obtained. She demanded something, and the German money,

140

representing the inflation at the turn of the century, was finally chosen in desperation. It is a joke—hopefully a pardonable one. The lady, it seems, could not care a fig, despite the huge denominations.

For a long time the German bisques were out of favor with collectors. Fine, costly specimens as well as character dolls were classified with the cheaper dolls as poor relations to the French *bébés*, and vulgar relations at that. This, of course, was a shortsighted judgment. The German bisques with socket heads and ball-jointed, strung bodies are certainly modeled after the style that originated in France, but there are other dolls with interesting and imaginative innovations that say a great deal for German inventiveness.

As for vulgarity, there is a time lag at work, the taste of the 1900's seeming vulgar and abhorrent from the viewpoint of the 1930's. It is amusing that the same dolls of 1900, unchanged, today seem fresh and delightful and are again in fashion. Amusing too are the reactions of an extremely young German artist, looking at a group of old dolls for the first time. In a complete reversal of taste, controlled by the time lag of her own generation, she thought the French *bébés* tasteless and vulgar and the German characters enchanting; she saved her abhorrence to heap on the 1930 celluloids.

Plate 22 depicts a group of eleven character dolls made by the Heubach Brothers, an established porcelain factory of Thüringen. The Heubachs made other china objects, and the heads of the dolls can sometimes be recognized in the figurines of children which the factory made in quantity. Whether the dolls were adapted from the figurines or designed concurrently is as yet conjecture. Certainly there is an interesting lesson in aesthetics here, just as there was when we put the bisque head in the china cabinet in Chapter 8; in the case of the Heubachs, the figurines, however actively the children are portrayed, are static and stilted beside the doll that has the same head, even though the doll can do no more than sit stiffly, his limbs dangling.

The dolls in this photograph are not in the least static or stiff. On the contrary, they seem to be bursting with life and laughter. They are modeled after real children, and from them

141

we get a very vivid glimpse of childhood in Germany in the early twentieth century. There are family likenesses to be found, and sometimes the same child can be recognized, a little older or in a different mood.

The fat boy with the bib and the gurgling baby have heads that are also found on figurines. The ridiculous pink and blue toddlers are mechanical, trundling across the floor with much shrill crying and waving of arms. The boy with the gray checked suit is from the same family, but his inset glass eyes and lamb's-wool wig give him a very different look. Rarest, perhaps, are the two large, solemn-faced children in the background; the loveliest is the laughing baby in the chair, her lacy pink bonnet molded to her head. The boy with the wig is from the collection of Maureen Popp. The others are from the collections of Margaret Whitton and the author.

There are many different inventions to be found among the German dolls of the early twentieth century, and they are often categorized for convenience, although occasionally the categories will cross. There are "character" children, babies, soldiers, ethnic dolls by race, color, or costume, and so on. From this plethora, clown dolls have been chosen for Plate 23. As many different types as possible were crowded into the picture—although many more were left out—in order to give some hint of their variety and the teeming imaginations of the doll-makers of that time.

The large clown with the "cat-in-the-box" has an ordinary bisque head, upon which the clown makeup was painted before the firing. The red clown in the rigging has a composition head, the fascinating detail here being the animal decals that were applied to his cheeks. The two tall clowns with cymbals are mechanical. Their hard plaster heads make these dolls look much older than they are. The harpist is also mechanical and is made of tin with a celluloid head modeled from a bisque one. The clown in the center has a pretty bisque head, which could have been made for a little-girl doll. The striped clown and absurd midget are fairground favors, cheaply made from plaster and cotton. The midget shoots out his tongue when he is squeezed.

Perhaps the most unusual dolls here are the jumping jack

in the rigging, with his subtly molded smiling bisque head, and
the violinist, who seems to be of the same, or at least very
similar, manufacture. His head is modeled with emphatic conviction and vitality, and his wooden body is fully articulated.
The clown with the decaled face, the harpist, the clown with
the "cat-in-the-box," and the fairground midget are from the
collection of Kit Robbins. The others are from the author's
collection.

Lady doll made by Simon and Halbig, of Germany, and dressed as a peasant of the Groningen province. The metal cap signifies a married woman. (*Coleman Collection*)

A lady doll, c. 1910, by Simon and Halbig, of a later period than the one shown on page 144. The modeling is impressionistic, and the whole concept of the doll is more sophisticated. (E. J. Carter Collection)

Marie Constable, with some of her birthday toys, in the summer of 1895. Her boots seem a sad imposition in hot weather, but the atmosphere is more relaxed than any we have encountered since the early 1800's (see the woodcut from *The Daisy* on page 21). Many of her toys can be identified; notice the tin "Bath Room" with its little bathing doll ready for its ablutions. (*Constable McCracken Archive, Museum of the City of New York*)

"The Children's Teaparty," a card for the stereopticon, made in 1900. This is a contrived picture, but it does show us real children at play. (*Author's Collection*)

A bisque shoulder-head by Simon and Halbig, representing a lady, extremely delicately modeled, as are the arms and hands of the doll to which it belongs (*Maureen Popp Collection*)

"Baby," the famous character doll that was adapted from a bronze bust by the German firm of Kammer and Reinhardt and marketed in 1909. Three different models are shown here, including the unusual Negro version, with its flocked hair. (*Kit Robbins Collection*)

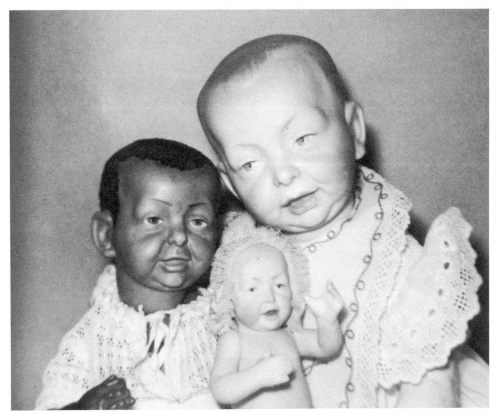

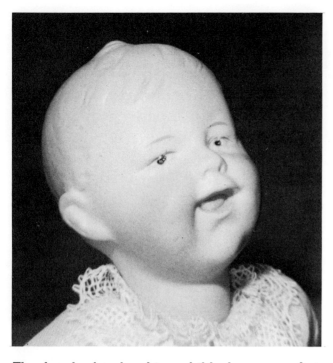

The head of a laughing child—here a socket head for a jointed doll—by Heubach Brothers, marked with the square mark and the figures "79/11." The company also made a figurine with the same head. (*Kit Robbins Collection*)

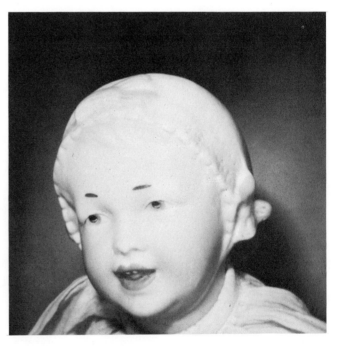

A doll's head representing a baby in a be-ribboned bonnet, all in bisque, made in the manner of the Heubach dolls (*Margaret Whitton Collection*)

CHAPTER 12

American Classics

Comparatively few dolls were produced in America during the nineteenth century. Most of them were regional products that did not attempt to compete with the great quantities of mass-produced dolls imported from Europe. Such dolls have for the most part a curiously insular quality; they came into being sometimes as the result of some isolated person's creative drive, as was the case with the Walker rag dolls. Elsewhere conventional European dolls were translated into more available materials, such as metal, rawhide, and rubber—sometimes as a side product of a larger industry.

The dolls made by the India Rubber Comb Company of New York may be cited here, and examples are shown in Plate 24. Their rubber heads are mounted on cloth bodies with leather hands, and they are both marked alike on the backs of their necks with the legend "I.R. Comb Co." The doll on the right has been much played with; her paint has flaked and been carefully patched at some time in her past. The doll on the left is in incredibly immaculate condition. Both dolls were made during the 1870's, and both wear their original clothes.

It was not unusual for a company making a doll for the first time, especially when it was only a sideline, to make their mold from an available commercial doll. Our India Rubber Comb Company dolls, however, are completely original work, with intricately arranged hair and fresh, thoughtful modeling. The density of the rubber gives a slightly turgid but curiously attractive quality to the molding, and this is offset by the light, impressionistic style of painting. There is nothing frivolous about these dolls; they are as deliberate and substantial as corn bread. The doll on the left is from the collection of Margaret Whitton. The doll on the right is from the collection of Maureen Popp.

With the turn of the century American doll-making gathered momentum. Ideas began to spring up like mushrooms, and new dolls appeared to tumble over each other as they tried to reach the rapidly expanding market. Many fine doll-makers became established during the early years of the twentieth century; some of their dolls were so original and pace-setting that they can with confidence be called classics. Their impact was immense on both the industry and the public alike.

Plate 25a shows a group of such dolls, the "All-Wood Perfection Art Dolls" of Albert Schoenhut, an immigrant from Germany whose family had been doll-makers for over a century. The Schoenhut dolls had solid wooden heads, which were molded under pressure and painted with enamel colors. The hollow bodies were contrived with elaborate interior steel springs, enabling the dolls to hold any pose indefinitely.

They appeared in 1911, alongside the new German character dolls with which they have much in common, in a market surfeited with the cheaper, vacuously smiling bisques from Germany. Their impact was enormous. The dolls in Plate 25a are tradesmen's samples, dressed in their original clothes. They have never been played with. Their free, lifelike quality is immediately apparent, as is their oddly mixed pedigree. They seem distinctly Germanic when compared with the Heubachs in Plate 22. Yet there is an air of newness and alertness, a freedom about them, a bouncing vitality that is wholly Amer-

150

ican. They are second-generation immigrants, preserved for posterity.

The doll on the extreme right, with his molded hair and mischievous smile, is called Schnickel-Fritz; he is one of Schoenhut's earlier masterpieces. The serious child with the molded bonnet is as rare as she is beautiful. The delightful animals are from the elaborate "Humpty Dumpty Circus," which was copyrighted by Schoenhut in 1903 and which stayed at the top of the toy market for thirty years. This enviable group is from the collection of Margaret Whitton.

The famous Kewpie dolls of Rose O'Neill began as decorations for the magazine stories that she illustrated in the early 1900's. In her book, *The One Rose*, Rowena Ruggles tells us that Rose's memories of a beloved baby brother were her inspiration and she quotes from Rose's own writings: "His starfish hands stretched out to reach your heart. . . . He was a shy little cherub with wings just sprouting."* So wrote Miss O'Neill, and she told her editor: "I have for a long time called these persons Kewpies, diminutive for Cupids, and it seems to me that the name, spelled so, might be amusing to children." And so the Kewpie pages appeared, first in 1909 in *Ladies' Home Journal* and subsequently in *Woman's Home Companion*, *Good Housekeeping*, and the *Delineator*. They were enormously successful and were followed by paper dolls, which Rose called her Kewpie Kutouts.

By 1913 a bisque Kewpie doll had been modeled by Rose O'Neill and was already being produced by more than twenty factories in Germany, all turning out Kewpies, according to Rose, "as fast as they could pull them out of the ovens."† She was extremely fussy about the quality of these dolls, and she even visited the factories in order to meet the workers personally. The result is exquisite, sugary perfection: Every eyelash is light and feathery, and even the pinpoint highlights of the eyes are placed exactly in order to produce the roguish twinkle that Rose intended.

Kewpies were soon being made in many other materials

---

* Rowena Godding Ruggles, *The One Rose* (Oakland, Calif.: Privately printed, 1964).

† *Ibid.*

and were applied to every type of merchandise. As might be expected, they were widely pirated, and cheap imitations have done the Kewpies a grave disservice. Outrageous as they were in many respects, Rose O'Neill's creations were never blatant or vulgar. At the same time, there was nothing halfhearted about them; they were frankly sentimental, as cloying as baby talk. They were also, in the most innocent and disarming way possible, erotic. They have the naïve sensuality of very small children who love to be kissed and cuddled, who respond with natural voluptuousness to the caresses of sunshine and water, the smoothness of feathers, and the richness of fur.

This, of course, is partly the secret of their universal appeal and is the reason that so many grown-ups find them irresistible. Rose herself adored them, multiplying them delightedly, inventing ever-fresh adventures, and building for them an elaborate, make-believe town, "Kewpieville." It is significant that many of the popular Kewpie items—clock cases, lamps, ashtrays, inkwells, Kewpie jewelry made of ivory and silver— were in essence items for the adult market. Even the ubiquitous "position Kewpies," or "action Kewpies," were figurines, many of them with a minor useful function, such as match-holding.

Plate 25b shows a group of these "action Kewpies," chosen not so much to show the great variety of subjects and occupations found among them but rather to illustrate how easy they are to play with, how readily they will start off on adventures. Two of the Kewpies here have been applied to adult, household objects: The smaller mandolin player sits on a bottle stopper, and the horizontal Kewpie reclines on a hamper-shaped trinket box. They are inspiring to photograph, and one longs to surround them with a shimmering palace of soap bubbles. In lieu of this they were given pastel silk and the ghosts of rosebuds. The Kewpie dolls are from the author's collection.

Rose O'Neill was not the only illustrator of this period whose pictures were made into dolls. Grace Weiderseim, who later became Grace Drayton by a second marriage in midcareer, created her own extraordinary world of childhood, quite different from Kewpieville. While Rose's fantastic creatures are frivolous and fey and light as thistledown, Grace's little people are earthbound. Gawky and clumsy, they stare at us in wide-eyed astonishment, toddlers who cannot tie their own shoe-laces or cope with their own coat buttons. This is childhood observed from an adult standpoint, tolerant and amused. One doubts whether children really understand it.

This is nothing new. Throughout the history of children's literature there are very few books, rare and precious indeed, written by authors who were themselves childlike and whose work in consequence is directly comprehensible to children. In one's own childhood there was a sharp if inexplicable awareness of this distinction; there were one's "special favorite books," and there were the others. *Alice in Wonderland, The Wind in the Willows*, the Peter Rabbit books, and the Christopher Robin books are a few that pass with flying colors.

Children notice but do not mind. They are both uncritical and voracious, and their books are all well fingered. In a way there is even something mysterious and exciting for children about books that they cannot really understand—books like those of Kate Greenaway, which at first seem to be meant for them but which really presuppose a knowledge and sophistication that they could not possibly possess.

Grace Drayton was prolific. Books and magazine items, postcards and comic strips, tumbled from her desk in profusion. Her paper dolls of Dolly Dingle and her friends appeared in the *Pictorial Review* for over twenty years. Perhaps her most famous toys are the "Campbell Kids," based on the advertisements she designed for the canned soup, which were known and loved everywhere. The Campbell Kids dolls were put out as a promotion and were so successful that they were reissued time and time again for successive generations. A version of them is still being made today.

Great quantities of such toys were marketed, but they were not made to last, and comparatively few survive. The doll in Plate 26a is remarkable in that it is unsold stock—or a manufacturer's sample—and is thus as clean and fresh as new, its label still on its wrist. It represents Bobby Bounce, the hero of one of Grace's storybooks, and is doubly remarkable in that it is the only example of this doll that we have so far been able to trace. In the background is one of the heavy babies' dishes that were decorated with Grace Drayton pictures. Together they admirably sum up the absurdity and charm of her world. Both items are from the collection of Rebecca Popp.

The perky little boys in Plate 26b are an unusual instance of a doll that started out as a work of art. Helen Jensen, a sculptress living in California, made a portrait bust of her little son in the early 1920's, which was cast in bronze and exhibited under the title "Laughing Child." An imaginative doll-maker persuaded Mrs. Jensen that the bust would make a wonderful doll, and "Gladdie" appeared in the toy shops shortly thereafter, with a cloth body and composition limbs. The larger doll in the photograph has the composition head, beautifully painted in oil colors and with stationary glass eyes. This head has a flange neck and is marked, "Copyright by H. Jensen, Germany."

The smaller doll has a similar construction, except that the head here is made of bisque. The equally careful coloring is fired into the china, producing a very different texture as well as a different scale of colors. There are other striking differences, caused by the nature of the media—the bisque, for instance, shrinks in the course of firing and may easily warp a little, subtly changing the expression of a face, whereas the imprecise texture of the composition softens and blurs the finer detail. The bisque head is very rare. It was made at a time when the German factories were at the end of their decline, and many difficulties and delays were encountered. Finally the bisque was abandoned in favor of the composition head. We are fortunate indeed to be able to present both dolls here. The larger doll is from the author's collection; the smaller doll with the bisque head is from Margaret Whitton's collection.

154

Plate 17. German fancy-bisque doll heads, c. 1870–1875

Plate 18a.
French china lady dolls, c. 1860

Plate 18b.
French china lady dolls,
perhaps by Maison Huret, c. 1860

Plate 19a. French bisque lady doll
with articulated wooden body,
c. 1875

Plate 19b.
French bisque lady dolls,
c. 1870–1875

157

Plate 20. French *bébés*, c. 1880

Plate 21. French *bébés* Jumeau, c. 1890

Plate 22. German bisque dolls by Heubach Brothers, c. 1905

Plate 23. German clown dolls, c. 1900–1920

Plate 24. American rubber-headed dolls,
made by the India Rubber Comb Company, c. 1875

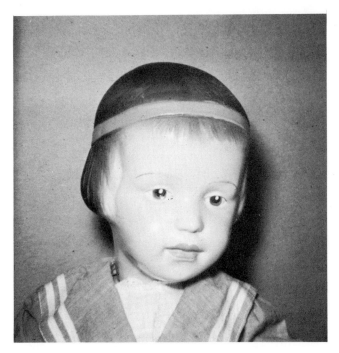

A gentle Schoenhut girl with unusual molded hair (*Kit Robbins Collection*)

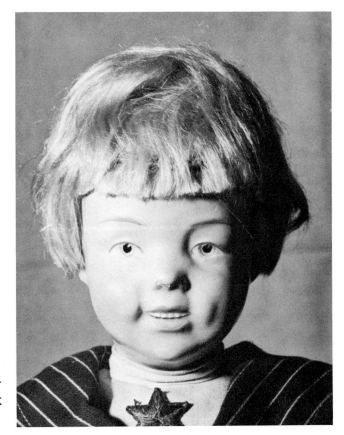

A close-up of a laughing Schoenhut boy, showing the distinctive modeling and brushwork (*Margaret Whitton Collection*)

A large and very handsome ringmaster doll, from the Schoenhut "Humpty Dumpty Circus" (Margaret Whitton Collection)

A valentine by Ernest Nister, of London, postmarked 1910. The artist responsible for "The Knight of the Violet" may not have been directly influenced by Rose O'Neill, but he was certainly working in the same artistic climate. (Author's Collection)

To My Valentine.

The Knight of the Violet

Cupid's ready for the fray,
Love will conquer you to-day.

Dear Kewp:
Accept this heart of mine
And take me for your
Valentine.

Kewpie valentines, designed by Rose O'Neill in about 1918 (*Kit Robbins Collection*) © J.L.K.

The Kewpies make love so wondrous fine,
They talk just like a Valentine,
I overheard them "bill and coo,"
And wrote this Valentine for you.

Three Kewpie derivatives—the Red Cross
officer and the policeman are bisque,
the soldier celluloid—marked "Japan"
(*Author's Collection*) © J.L.K.

A clock case in bisque, imitating Jasper
ware, with dancing Kewpies (*Margaret
Whitton Collection*) © J.L.K.

A Kewpie, designed to hold talcum powder. Two specimens are shown here, one in its original box. (*Kit Robbins Collection*) © J.L.K.

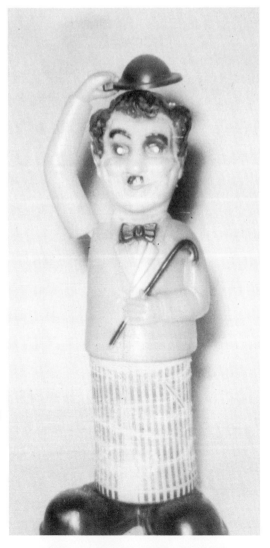

Charlie Chaplin in celluloid: a modern plastic mechanical toy from Italy (*Kit Robbins Collection*)

"Charlie McCarthy," the toy ventriloquist's doll that was marketed in the 1930's (*Kit Robbins Collection*)

"Jiggs," a jointed metal doll portraying one of the characters in the famous comic strip "Bringing Up Father" (*Albert Eisenlau Collection*)

"W. C. Fields," a portrait doll made by Effanbee in the early 1930's, a speaking likeness in more ways than one. The composition head is made in the manner of ventriloquists' dolls, the jaw being moved by a wire in the back of the neck. (*Kit Robbins Collection*)

CHAPTER 13

Rarities and Mysteries

The study of old dolls is not a cut-and-dried matter. Despite their proliferation, children's toys, even expensive ones, are seldom considered important objects by their makers, and their documentation is often fragmentary. When facts do exist, their significance is often clouded by the lore and legend added by well-meaning but amateur collectors. Since we know so little about so many dolls, it is not surprising that there are a few dolls about which nothing seems to be known.

Several such dolls were encountered while gathering the material for this book. Some of them are of recognizable origins yet do not lend themselves to categorization. Also, there are those rare variants of standard dolls which proved either impractical or unprofitable and were discontinued before they could reach the market in very large numbers. Others simply exist, their presence unexplained by any known archive or family record. For the researcher such mysteries are provocative and exciting, and the rarities have, of course, a will-o'-the-wisp allure for the collector. A few of these dolls are presented here: the small, irreducible nucleus that, one feels, must at all costs be included. They could have been tacked on as appendages to appropriate chapters, but it seems more fitting to spotlight them, a glittering company, the rarest and most fascinating.

Plate 27a shows the first of this elite company: a doll that is unique, as far as can be discovered. It has a head of waxed papier-mâché with simple black-pupiled eyes and a molded headdress. Real hair has been added, fastened about this headdress as though it were growing from beneath it. The body is made of stuffed muslin with leather arms; the dress is modern. Dolls of this type were made in Germany during the 1860's and 1870's in a wide variety of styles. More commonly they were made with molded hair, but none of them are plentiful. The doll here is an unusually large and splendid example.

The little flat cap, set quite straight and tied under the chin, is worn over a pure, classical coiffure with a bunch of long curls falling from the center of the high knot. This exact arrangement is to be found in the fashion plates and portraits of about 1805. It disappeared entirely by 1820, and nothing like it is to be found again until the Regency revival of the 1890's. The Greek knots and mobcaps of that "greenery-yallery" mode have a self-conscious quaintness quite unlike the chaste simplicity that we see here. By that time too, such dolls were no longer made except for a few cheap and poorly made stragglers.

So here is a delightful enigma. Some contend that the doll has to be from the 1870's, whatever it wears on its head; others feel that the extraordinary accuracy of the headdress could only be achieved in about 1805 while the fashion was still contemporary, in which case the doll is, or should be, technically impossible. This doll is from the collection of Margaret Whitton.

The doll in Plate 27b is very rare. This is a *bébé* made by Maison Huret in the 1880's. We have already examined more-typical examples of the work of this great doll-maker, which was at its zenith in the early 1860's. We can only conjecture about the impetus that produced this remarkable latecomer, marveling at her distinctive character as we wonder at her beauty. This doll is from the collection of Maureen Popp.

172

There are no doubts whatever about the origin of the mechanical doll in Plate 28. It is clearly marked (one is tempted to say signed) by Alexandre Théroude, a French toy-maker famous for his fine mechanicals. This seems to be an early example, perhaps from the 1850's. The extraordinary thing about this doll is its condition; except for the hole in the overskirt, it is as perfect as when it was first made: The paint on the papier-mâché head is smooth and unscratched, the kid arms are spotless, and the clothes are fresh and glittering. The mechanism is in perfect order too, and the doll, when set in motion, moves in a wide, stately circle, raising her hands alternately and turning her head to smell her bouquet as she proceeds. The costume is another charming attempt at chinoiserie, and one is tempted to place her in Chapter 7 with the other Oriental extravagances. She is extremely beautiful, however, and richly deserves her special place. This doll is from the collection of Fanchon Canfield.

By the same token, the two dolls shown on page 177 could easily have been added to the chapter on French ladies, although each alone is unusual enough to be worthy of this chapter. Together they are extraordinary. Ethnic dolls, as we have seen, were not made by the European factories with any seriousness until the turn of the century. Among French lady dolls of the 1860's and 1870's they are not at all common. Occasionally a standard head is found, tinted to represent the dusky skin of an Indian or mulatto lady; such dolls are usually in regional costumes. Here, however, the usual French features have been modified to represent the characteristic facial structure of the Negro.

The little doll on the right is very black indeed, and the enamel has a high gloss that, like the hair on some fancy bisque heads, could be mistaken for a glaze. The gussetted kid body is equally black. The head swivels on a shoulder plate; the modeling of the Negroid features is subtle and delicate, and the expression is very gentle. The taller doll is chocolate-colored, the kid body matching the bisque exactly. The head is molded in one piece with the shoulders, and there is a beautifully sculpted bosom. The open mouth with its slightly irregular teeth is very personal; the head is poised and dignified.

Such heads are found, rarely, on musical or mechanical dolls. For them to be made up as lady dolls is remarkable indeed. Both dolls have been redressed recently, with considerable panache.

Plate 29 shows examples of dolls that are portraits of a silent-movie star, made a quarter of a century before such toys became commonplace. Both dolls are rarities, and it is amusing that they represent different aspects of Charlie Chaplin's personality with remarkable accuracy.

The doll on the right is a lifelike portrait not only of the wistful screen character but also of the handsome, virile actor who created him. It is a surprising head to find on an inexpensive doll. Notice the oversized, oddly characterized feet.

The mechanical toy is much more expensive, although the composition head and the costume bear so slight a resemblance to the comedian that one wonders if it really is meant to be Charlie (or Charlot, more properly, since this toy is French). When the key is wound, however, the character is unmistakable. There is that nervous shuffle, that apologetic, rocking gait. The cane swings on his arm; we expect him to raise his hat with staccato politeness. Between the two dolls, a vivid impression of the great comedian is preserved. The portrait doll is from the Coleman collection; the mechanical is from the Museum of the City of New York.

The "Rose Pierrette" in Plate 30 is an unusual example of the boudoir dolls of the 1920's, which were intended to sit decoratively on beds and dressing tables. It is not a child's toy, but it is nevertheless a doll. Like mascots and other toys made for adults at that time, it is an example of a significant trend toward make-believe and regression. This feminine attitude is still part of our culture today, and we perhaps are not aware of its oddness. We have only to imagine a young lady of 1850 or 1870 with a collection of plush animals to see the incongruity. In these earlier periods dolls were certainly possessed by ladies, tricked up prettily as pincushions, hair tidies, and so on, but although such dolls were decorative, they were subservient to their functions, objects to be used and not to be played with.

Boudoir dolls have so far been ignored by serious collectors. This is partly because those that survive are often shabby, and there is little to commend them to the preserving impulse. The nostalgia of lost childhood is not there, and because they were once so fashionable, they quickly became old-fashioned and contemptible. When they are found in good condition, however, they provide a penetrating glimpse of the taste of the twenties and thirties.

The doll pictured in Plate 30 is a superior lady indeed, made for an exclusive modiste on the Faubourg St. Honoré in Paris, an expensive and trifling delectation for bored customers. She has been preserved in immaculate condition. This pierrette is dressed fancifully as a red rose, and the first thing we notice about her is that she is very red indeed—the color is brilliant and singing and is obviously no ordinary dye. The costume is wittily fashioned from the parts of the flower; the bodice and limb coverings represent tenuous stems, whereas the skirt and neck ruffle are contrived from petals. The doll is made entirely by hand. The long dangling legs and gesturing arms are skillfully stuffed and shaped, a difficult task on such a small scale. The face is shaped with stitches and then covered with silk crepe. The painted features are done with considerable verve. This doll is fantastic and chic and has been realized with great restraint. She reminds us suddenly of the disciplined, pared-down designs of Edmund Dulac, who would not have been ashamed of her. In her own frivolous way, she is sculpture in fabric. This doll is from the author's collection.

Plate 31a offers a mystery indeed. It is not unusual for a marked doll to remain unidentified, even when the mark proclaims the country of origin. It is, however, extraordinary to find a fine and unusual doll, so marked, of which almost no other examples are known. On the back of the head of this beautiful boy doll is incised: "N.T.I. Made in England." At the time of writing, the factory issuing this mark has not been traced, and although the doll is such a fine product that one would expect to find many other examples, very few others have so far been found with this same mark.

The mystery deepens as we examine the doll. He is quite late, perhaps even from the 1920's, and he is made with great sophistication. The bisque is fine quality; the modeling is sensitive. The head is painted with extraordinary bravura and the cheeks not tinted so much as splashed with a distinctive high-

175

keyed pink. The brows and lashes are done with a striking flourish to match the ebullience of the carefully tousled hair. The sum of this carefully calculated detail is the very essence of boyhood.

It is incredible that this spectacular doll was not enormously popular; but successes, as we have seen, survive in great numbers, and this boy, as far as we know at present, is almost the only one of his kind that exists today. It is from the collection of Maureen Popp.

To conclude this chapter fittingly, we have the doll in Plate 31b, of which nothing is known whatsoever. He is without precedent, a doll mystery unlike anything encountered before. He is extremely beautiful. His head is like heroic sculpture reduced in scale; the features of a young boy are professionally modeled with panache and with great realism. The paint—a very thick oil color, almost an impasto—is done in perfect harmony. It is impossible to say what material this doll is made of; the treatment suggests wood, although it seems very light in weight and may be hollowed.

The head is mounted on a German jointed body of good quality, made in the early 1900's, and the carefully tailored evening clothes with the faultless linen are from the same period. There is an astonishing vitality and strength of character, a sense of rapt concentration and of power contained. Is he a portrait? One longs to know more but can only admire —and covet. This doll is from the collection of Bess Goldfinger.

Two French lady dolls, representing black women. They are not alike but are both unusual in that the conventional French heads have been modified with the characteristic facial structure of the Negro races. (*Fanchon Canfield and Margaret Whitton Collections*)

Two laughing little Moors, marked "S.F.B.J.,"
based on a boy doll produced by this company with several variations. The skin color is
charcoal black, and the hair is flocked. The
Algerian costumes are ethnically accurate, both
in fabric and in color. (*Sylvia Brockman Collection*)

A whimsical little waxed-papier-mâché boy, his
hat molded with his head. He is done in the
technique and has something of the manner of
the doll in Plate 27a. This doll is from the last
quarter of the nineteenth century. (*Margaret
Whitton Collection*)

A very rare mechanical doll. This is a variant on the Goodwin patent of 1868; such toys were made by other companies under license, and they can be found with a variety of carriages, different heads, and so on. This is the only example, to our present knowledge, in which an occupant for the carriage was provided by the maker. (*Margaret Whitton Collection*)

An extremely rare mechanical made by Vichy, of Paris, in the 1850's.
As the horse gallops, the Arab doll rocks in his saddle, firing his rifle
and jerking his head fiercely. (*Margaret Whitton Collection*)

Some unusual French mechanicals. The flute and drum player has a Jumeau head; his clothes and mechanism are all original and perfect. The waltzing couple performs a most elaborate series of steps in time to its own concealed music box. (*Dorothy Blankley and Fanchon Canfield Collections*)

A very rare papier-mâché man doll, with molded cap and whiskers. It is dressed in a homemade young boy's suit, not removable, beneath which is an earlier costume. Loose strips of calico are sewn to a base in a fish-scale pattern, and the legs are similarly covered. In their book, *Dolls and Dolls' Houses*, Estrid Faurholt and Flora Gill Jacobs reproduce a page from a German toy dealer's catalog of the 1840's, showing two variants of this head on dolls dressed as harlequins in the suit of stylized multicolored rags which was worn by Arlecchino in the early commedia dell'arte and from which has evolved the more familiar suit of lozenge-shaped patches. (*Margaret Whitton Collection*)

A Jumeau doll obviously specially made for an exhibit and dressed to represent Eleanor of Austria, who became the wife of Francis I of France. The doll is large and handsome, made like the French ladies but with a very unusual head. The exhibition label came with the doll; unfortunately, it is not dated. (*E. J. Carter Collection*)

CHAPTER 14

Second Time Around

Dolls are not always the exclusive province of children. In this concluding chapter some remarkable dolls that have nothing whatever to do with children are examined. They are made today specifically for collectors and are properly known as the doll-artist dolls. They are not made in factories or in any way as commercial products. Theirs is an amateur field in the finest sense of the word. These dolls are made for the most part at home, as a hobby or a relaxation from some other employment, by creative, talented people who themselves are often doll collectors. Such dolls are intended to be prized and cherished as works of art, and they are often made in limited editions, like etchings or lithographs. Occasionally they are one of a kind.

Precedents for these adult toys are to be found in the shell-work dolls and peddlers of the mid-nineteenth century and in the "art" dolls popular about 1900. The clear concept of the doll artist did not emerge until the late 1920's, however, when there were enough organized collectors to create a demand for them. This is essentially an American phenomenon, although the rapidly growing interest in doll-collecting in other countries is certain to foster doll-artists in other parts of the world.

Meanwhile the ranks of the American doll-artists are swelling, and although their work is notably individual in character, it is possible in surveying them to arrive at some generalizations. For instance, there is a decided preference for traditional techniques and materials—wood, wax, and, predominantly, porcelain bisque. It is curious that this last medium should be so popular, for it is the most complicated, requiring a number of skills and elaborate equipment. Nevertheless, more doll-artists seem to work in bisque than in any other medium. The subject matter of these dolls is interesting, since it unconsciously reflects popular American attitudes and tastes. It is possible to generalize here too, and we find that the dolls seem to fall mostly into two major categories, each of them an extension of a desirable type of antique doll.

First, there are dolls representing children or babies. These a layman might easily mistake for play dolls intended for children. They take their inspiration from the French *bébés* and the German character dolls, and they are often conceived with a good deal of wit and imagination.

Among the finest of these dolls are the enchanting children made by Ellery Thorpe. In design and structure Mrs. Thorpe's dolls are as traditional as the fine bisque from which the heads and limbs are made. In personality, however, they are like no others; once you have discovered them you will always recognize them. They are extremely lifelike—indeed, they brim with vitality. If not actually portraits, they are certainly modeled from nature, a synthesis of real children whom the artist knows and loves.

Two of Ellery Thorpe's toddlers, costumed by her, are pictured on page 189. They are called Mischief and Michael. Their excellence is immediately apparent. It is interesting to note how subtly they are designed. For instance, Mischief's high spirits concentrate in the sparkle of her deep-set blue glass eyes; Michael's tear-dimmed gaze, all turbulence and outrage, is better conveyed by his painted eyes. In these little dolls Ellery Thorpe has captured vividly the fleeting joys and sorrows of childhood. It is impossible not to respond to them, and it is surely significant that of all the dolls in this book, these were the easiest to arrange. Commercial dolls of this kind are all too often slick and cloyingly sentimental. Here is proof that in the hands of a sensitive artist such dolls can be fresh, original, and delightfully human.

Our second category of doll-artist dolls takes its inspiration from the lady dolls of the past, especially the German fancy bisques of the 1860's and 1870's, with their molded hairstyles and headgear. Portraits of famous women of history are by far the most popular subjects. The intention is decidedly ambitious, and the dolls are often grandiose. At the same time they are oddly static, more like elaborately dressed figurines. Nevertheless, they are intended as dolls, and they conform to our definition of a doll as a plaything, since the very acts of creating, collecting, and preserving them constitute play on a very elevated and gratifying scale.

The work of one artist in this category, the late Martha Thompson, achieves a level of excellence unrivaled anywhere. Many of her dolls are historical portraits; they were made after careful research and with remarkable insight into the characters of her subjects. Imbued with a strong sense of decoration, Martha Thompson loved to confect rich details for her creations. She used a porcelain clay that she composed herself, very smooth and fine grained, and that she controlled with seeming effortlessness. She could give it the texture of velvet or rough straw, she could spin it into airy ruffles or flying ribbons. These decorations were always used to emphasize the character of the doll, and although they are often elaborate, they do not predominate. With all her virtuosity, Martha Thompson understood and respected her clay; she never abused it or strained its capabilities.

An example of her finest work can be seen in Plate 32, her portrait of Anne of Cleves, based on the contemporary painting by Hans Holbein. Here is a monumental dignity that defeats our sense of scale, making the doll seem larger than life —it is in fact scarcely one foot high. The entire headdress is molded in porcelain, providing rich strata of textures: the pliant skin, the burnished-gold caul, the smooth linen hood,

187

and finally the headdress itself, heavy and jewel encrusted.

Yet all this splendor is dominated and made secondary by the noble head, which for all its delicacy is handled with a breadth exactly geared to the nature of the clay. The personality of the serene and enigmatic princess is perceived with such penetrating insight that we are brought up short, remembering that this is, after all, a doll. When we learn that it was made by a busy housewife in her snatched moments of leisure and on her kitchen table, we are awed and humbled.

This doll was costumed by Margaret Finch, and a tribute must be paid to skill of no small order. To control fabrics on this small scale is far from easy, yet the velvet and embroideries fall and fold as perfectly as if they were life-size. We do not realize just how skillful this costuming is until we discover that the jeweled collar and neckline, which match the porcelain headdress perfectly, are in fact made of stitchery and are part of the costume. The doll "Anne of Cleves" is from the collection of Margaret Whitton.

This has been a glimpse of the extraordinary achievements of two established doll-artists. There are many others whose dolls are personal, exciting, and meritorious. Today's collectors, especially those with modest resources, would be well advised to invest in their work, as fine antique dolls command such prohibitive prices. Depend on it: Today's doll-artist dolls are the costly antiques of tomorrow.

"Mischief" and "Michael," two brilliant portrait dolls by Ellery Thorpe
(*Margaret Whitton Collection*)

"La Duchesse de Longeville," a portrait doll taken from a painting, by Martha Thompson. Besides being extremely beautiful, this head is technically a tour de force, showing an astonishing mastery of the medium. (*Margaret Whitton Collection*)

A group of dolls by Martha Thompson, based on fashion plates of the 1830's. The freely modeled hair and lacy cap are made in the porcelain; on a head less than three inches high this is a remarkable achievement. (*Margaret Whitton Collection*)

Fashion plate of a gentleman's costume for the
late 1820's; Martha Thompson's man doll, shown
on page 191, is based on similar plate. (*Author's
Collection*)

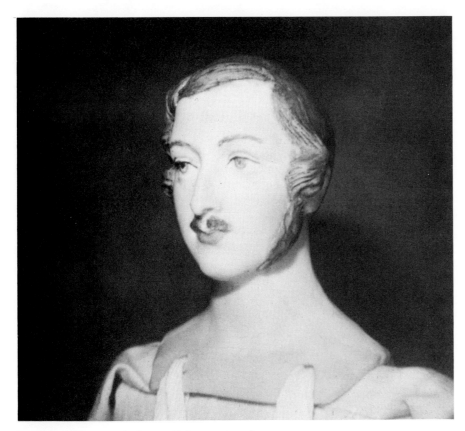

Prince Albert of Saxe-Coburg at the time of his marriage to Queen Victoria of England. This is the companion piece to Martha Thompson's portrait of the young queen. It shows her skill in capturing a likeness without exaggeration or mannerism, an especially remarkable achievement, as it was done in a refractory medium and on a very difficult scale. (*Author's Collection*)

A doll representing an old peasant woman, by Ada Odenreider. This unusual doll is beautifully made, the character portrayed with sensitivity and compassion. (*Bess Goldfinger Collection*)

Plate 25a.
American wooden dolls,
made by Albert Schoenhut, c. 1911

Plate 25b.
German-made bisque Kewpie dolls,
c. 1913, © J.L.K.

Plate 26a. "Bobby Bounce,"
an American composition doll,
designed by Grace Drayton,
c. 1910

Plate 26b. "Gladdie,"
two versions of an American doll,
designed by Helen Jensen, c. 1920

Plate 27a.
Waxed–papier-mâché doll
with molded headdress

Plate 27b.
French *bébé* made by Maison Huret,
c. 1885

Plate 28.
French mechanical doll, made by Alexandre Théroude,
c. 1855–1860

Plate 29.
French and American dolls, representing Charlie Chaplin,
c. 1910–1920

Plate 30. French boudoir doll, c. 1925

Plate 31a.
English bisque doll, c. 1920

Plate 31b.
Boy doll with painted head,
c. 1900–1910

201

Plate 32. "Anne of Cleves,"
a bisque portrait doll by Martha Thompson, c. 1960

Epilogue

In this book we have tried to look at old dolls with fresh eyes, to see them not through the glass of our cabinets or over our dealers' counters but as they were first seen by the parents who bought them and the children who received them. We have attempted to refocus upon the true identity of these old playthings, which of recent years is becoming alarmingly blurred and twisted.

This distortion, which is gradually devitalizing the impact of most dolls, is largely a matter of values. The prices fetched by old toys reach astonishing heights, and it is difficult to remember that the doll for which one has been searching for so long and for which one has had to pay so many hundreds of dollars was, to its original maker and purchaser alike, a fairly trivial matter. It is not surprising that a china doll's head takes on the importance of a rare porcelain when the purchase money would obtain a very handsome porcelain indeed.

Further falsification results from what is too often done to dolls by dealers and collectors. Shabby and broken examples are uneconomical, since perfect specimens fetch such a great deal of money, and it is worth the expense of having them "restored" to a salable condition.

And here is a sad distortion, since the doll's true value, as opposed to this false monetary one, is in the directness with which it has come down to us from the past. The less it has been disturbed, the more valuable it is. The collector, however, in all innocence, is apt to think that because the doll was so very expensive, it should look as complete and clean and perfect as possible. Consequently, the doll is repaired, remodeled, refired, rebuilt, re-covered, relimbed, rewaxed, repainted, rewigged, and re-dressed; and finally it is clamped on a stand, like a butterfly on a pin. All contact with the past

203

is destroyed and with it all of the doll's fascinating and sometimes unique insights into the life of another time, which were its most important asset.

This may sound like harsh criticism of a gentle and harmless hobby, but a little thought will show how dangerous these practices can be, especially when one remembers the extent to which they are now carried on. An exhibition of collectors' dolls is all too likely to reveal, besides many wonderful and unexpected treasures, a swamping tide of dolls that are all so distorted by the above processes that it is hard to realize they were ever old. They exist in a curious no-man's-land of "olden days," as pretty and frilly and senseless as the pictures on boxes of chocolates. The truth has been destroyed, the dolls debased into worthless parodies. As the demand increases and prices rise, the danger to the remaining dolls also increases.

Such distortions and debasements could be easily avoided if sufficient emphasis were placed on the importance of truth. We need only develop an awareness of the doll's relation to its original environment. The moment this is achieved, we become aware of a direct reversal of our values—and also of a paradox. The doll's value is now increased by its very fragility and by the ease with which its original state can be destroyed. And we realize with surprise that a battered doll in a crumbling dress could be a precious, even priceless, object, whereas the same doll "restored" is worthless. It cannot be emphasized too strongly that the aesthetic and historical value of the doll depends directly on the degree to which it has come down to us undisturbed except by the natural processes of decay.

If we turn to museums, we can see the value of conservation as opposed to restoration. Unless a well-meaning amateur has been allowed in with scissors, bleach bottle, and shampoo, the collections in museums, dusty and unheeded though they sometimes may be, are the last strongholds in which old dolls can be found untouched, since they were last played with, by anything but time.

The collection at Gunnersbury Park, outside London, comes vividly to mind. It not only bridges the gap in time but also presents the dolls to us with their vital essence intact. One is overwhelmed and one is pierced—not only by nostalgia but also by the recognition of truth. As we peer into unlit cupboards or lift venerable boxes from their shelves, the Victorian nursery is so close to us that we can even smell its bland, innocent aroma. The dolls—some perfect, some cracked and crumbling, with a limb missing here, a dress clumsily mended there—are so vibrantly complete that one is in awe of them.

This, to me, is the true meaning of original condition. Although it would be absurd to suggest that everyone should collect and treasure only grimy, mildewed wrecks on the strength of this premise, nevertheless these dolls will never have more aesthetic unity or historical importance than they do at this point.

It was with these convictions that this book was assembled. Every effort has been made to present each doll truthfully, using examples in their original state wherever possible. Their surroundings were chosen with care, and I have tried not to impose on the dolls my own personal concept of them. I hope they speak for themselves.

Index

The page numbers in italics refer to illustrations.

Adventures of Two Dutch Dolls, The (Upton), 17
Aladdin (pantomime), 84
"Albert of Saxe-Coburg, Prince" (doll), *193*
Alice in Wonderland (Carroll), 153
American dolls
    classics, 149–154, *163, 164, 167, 168, 169*
    first commercial, 31
    industry established, 150
    Kewpies, 151–152, *166, 167, 195*
    papier-mâché, 55–56, *93*
    primitives, 31–34
    rubber-headed, 149–150, *162*
    wooden, 150–151, *195*
Andersen, Hans Christian, 85
"Anne of Cleves" (doll), 187–188, *202*
Anstey, Christopher, 11
Arlecchino, 182
Art Nouveau, 101
Arts and Crafts movement, 107
Austen, Jane, 13, 15
Austria, doll manufacture in, 3

"Baby" (doll), *147*
"Baby with Doll" (Hamblin), 43
Badekinder, 56–57, *63, 64, 65, 93*
Beaman, H. G. Hulme, 17
Beauty, valued points of, 9
Bébés (dolls), 125–129, *131,* 132, 133, *134,*
        136, *138, 158, 159,* 172, *197*
    body of, 125
    compared with German bisques, 141
    confusion with French dolls, 128–129
    extravagance of, 126
    popularity of, 125–126
Belton dolls, 127, *158*
Berlin Exhibition of 1844, 47
Bisque dolls, 125, 126, 128, *147, 148,* 150,
        154, *166,* 176, 186, *201, 202*
    and emergence of composition, 154
    French china, 114–115, *117, 118, 120, 121,*
        123, 157
    hooded china, *98,* 100–101
    Oriental, 85, *88, 97*
    related to decorated chinaware, 89–90
    See also Fancy-bisque dolls; German bisque
        dolls
Blankley, Dorothy, 15, 85

"Bobby Bounce" (doll), 153, *196*
Boudoir dolls, 174–175, *200*
Boy doll with painted head, 176, *201*
"Bringing Up Father" (comic strip), 168
Bru Jne & Cie (doll-makers), 125, 128, 131
Burnett, Frances Hodgson, 17

"Campbell Kids" (dolls), 153
Canfield, Fanchon, 173
Carter, E. J., 16
Cézanne, Paul, 4
Champney, James Wells, 130
Charlie Chaplin dolls, *167,* 174, *199*
"Charlie McCarthy" (doll), *168*
Children, attitudes toward, 1–3
Children's Encyclopedia, 85
Children's Hour (radio program), 17
"Children's Teaparty, The" (stereopticon
        card), *146*
China dolls, 45–48, *58, 59, 60, 62*
    early commercial manufacture, 45
    See also French china dolls; German china
        dolls
Chinese dolls, *see* Oriental dolls
Chinoiserie, 83–85, 173
Chopin, Frédéric, 46
Christopher Robin books, 153
Classical influences, 21
Clement, Pierre Victor, 115
Clock case, *166*
Clown dolls, 142, *161*
Coiffures, elaborate, 27
Coleman collection, 5, 55, 70, 174
Coleridge, Samuel Taylor, 83
Collectors' dolls, *see* Doll-artist dolls
Collector's Encyclopedia of Dolls (Coleman),
        33
Composition dolls, 68–71, *73, 75, 77, 81, 95,*
        96, 172, *178, 196*
    emergence of, 154
Constable, Marie, *146*
Conte and Boehme (firm), 57
Copeland Parian ware, 103
"Cornelia Ward Hall and Her Children"
        (Gordigiani), *136*
Crane, Walter, 107
Cranford (Mitford), 16

Daisy, The (children's book), *21*
Davis, Frank, 83
Delineator (magazine), 151
Derby, Alberta, 56
Devis, Anthony, 7
Doll-artist dolls, 185–188, *189, 190, 191, 192, 193, 202*
  categories of, 186–187
  precedents for, 185–186
Dollhouses, 5, 16
Dolls and Dollmakers (Hillier), 57
Dolls and Dolls' Houses (Faurholt and Jacobs), 182
"Dolly Dingle" (paper doll), 153
Drayton, Grace, 152–154, 196
"Duchesse de Longeville, La" (doll), *190*
Dulac, Edmund, 175

Early, Alice, 3
Eastlake, Charles, 101
Eekhoff, R., 140
Effanbee (firm), 169
"Eleanor of Austria" (doll), *183*
Elssler, Fanny, *42,* 47, *50, 51*
Emperor and the Nightingale, The (Andersen), 85
England, doll manufacture in, 3
English bisque doll, 175–176, *201*
English Dolls, Effigies, and Puppets (Early), 3
"Ernest Fiedler Family, The" (Heinrich), 58
"Ethel" (doll), 115–116, *123*
Ethnic dolls, manufacture of, 173
Eugénie, Empress, 111

Fancies (dolls), *98,* 100–101
Fancy-bisque dolls, 89–90, *98, 99–101, 102, 103, 104, 105, 106, 107, 108, 109, 110, 155*
  compared to fancies, 100
  compared to hooded china dolls, 100
  earliest, 90
  misuse of "Parian" name for, 103
"Fanny Elssler" (doll), *42, 47–48*
Fashion plates, *22, 27, 117, 119, 120, 122, 132, 133, 135, 192*
Faurholt, Estrid, 182
Finch, Margaret, 188
Fleurs animées, Les (Grandville), 87
Fortune, Robert, 85
France, doll manufacture in, 3, 111
Francis I, King, 183
Franklin, Benjamin, 32
"Frederick" (doll), 115–116, *123*
French china dolls, 111–116, *156*
  bébés confused with, 128–129
  bisque, 114–115, *117, 118, 120, 121, 123, 157*
  contributing craftsmen, 111–112
  earliest examples, 112
  by Maison Huret, 113, *117, 156*
  mulatto, *121*

Gainsborough, Thomas, 5
Gautier, Théophile, 47
Gavarni, 46
Georgian period, 1–6, 15
German bisque dolls, *98,* 114, 139–143, *144, 145, 147, 148, 160, 161,* 187, 195
  compared with *bébés,* 141
  lifelike details, 140
  Oriental, 85, *88,* 97
German china dolls, *41, 42,* 53–54, *61,* 68, *91, 92*
  quantity of, 53
  representing children, 55, *92*
Germany, doll manufacture in, 3, 13, 17, 68
Gilbert and Sullivan, 85
Ginsberg, Cora, 6
"Girl in a Garden," *30*
"Gladdie" (doll), 154, *196*
Goldfinger, Bess, 19, 48, 55, 176
Good Housekeeping (magazine), 151
Gordigiani, Michael, 136
Grandville, J. J., 87
Greco-Roman influences, 20
Greenaway, Kate, 17, 128, 153
Greiner, Ludwig, 55
Grimms' Fairy Tales, 85
Gunnersbury Park collection, 204
Gutta-percha dolls, 54, 55

Heubach Brothers, 141, 148, 150, 160
Hillier, Mary, 57
Hoare, William, 11
Holbein, Hans, 187
Holland, doll manufacture in, 3
Hooded china dolls, *98,* 100–101
"House That Jack Built, The" (museum exhibit), *63*
"Humpty Dumpty Circus" (Schoenhut), 151, *164*

India Rubber Comb Company, 149, 150, *162*
Indian dolls, 173
Industrial Revolution, 3

Jacobs, Flora Gill, 182
Japanese dolls, *see* Oriental dolls
Jasper ware, imitation, 166
Jenkins, Mary, 4
Jensen, Helen, 154, 196
"Jiggs" (doll), *168*
Johl, Janet, 31
Johnson, Jacob, 21
"Jouets du jour de l'an, Les" (lithograph), *23*
Journal des enfants, Le (publication), 132
Jumeau (firm), 126, 129, 134, 137, 159, 183

Kammer and Reinhardt (firm), 147
Kewpie dolls, 151–152, *166, 167, 195*
Kewpie valentines, *165*

King, Rev. Joseph, 12
King, Mary, 12
Kittell, Nicholas Biddle, 49
"Knight of the Violet, The" (Nister), *164*

Ladies' Home Journal (magazine), 151
"Ladies of Distinction in Fashionable Dresses" (engraving), *21*
"Laughing Child" (Jensen), 154
Leuch's trade directory, 140
Liszt, Franz, 46

"Mademoiselle Catherina" (engraving), *9*
Maillol, Aristide, 4
Maison Huret (firm), 113, 117, 156, 172, 197
Marguerite dolls, 100, 101, *109, 110*
"Mary Jenkins" (doll), 4–5, 7, *35*
"Mary King" (doll), *12*
Metal dolls, 149
"Michael" (doll), 186–187, *189*
Mikado, The (Gilbert and Sullivan), 85
Minton (firm), 103
"Mischief" (doll), 186–187, *189*
"Mr. and Mrs. Charles Henry Carter" (Kittell), *49*
Mitford, Miss, 16
Moniteur de la mode, Le (publication), 117
Moor dolls, *178*
Motschmann (firm), 68, 73, 84
Mulatto dolls, *121*, 173
Murray, Mary King, 12
Museum of Humorous Taxidermy, 63
Museum of the City of New York, 5, 6, 16, 69, 71, 72, 84, 85, 99, 100, 113, 114, 115, 174

Negro dolls, 16, *38, 147*, 173–174, *177*
Nister, Ernest, 164

Odenreider, Ada, 193
One Rose, The (Ruggles), 151
O'Neill, Rose, 151–152, 164
Opium Wars, 85
Oriental dolls, 68–69, 83–85, *87, 97*, 102
   bisque, 85, *88, 97*

Papier-mâché dolls, 13–16, *20, 24, 25, 29, 37, 38*, 55–56, 68, *93, 182*
   disproportion in, 29
   first mass-production of, 13
   popularity of, 15
Parian ware, 103
Peddler dolls, 19, *38*
Pegwooden dolls, 16–19, *28, 38, 39*
   earliest, 17
Peter Rabbit books, 153
Pictorial Review (publication), 153
Popp, Maureen, 34, 129, 142, 150, 172, 176

Popp, Rebecca, 154
Poppe, Aug., 47, 48
Porcelain dolls, *see* China dolls
Potter, Mabel Gray, 115, 116, 123
Poured-wax dolls, 70–71, *78, 79, 80, 95, 96*
Prize, The (magazine), 75

Racketty-Packetty House (Burnett), 17
Rag dolls, 40, *44*
Rare and mysterious dolls, 171–176, *178, 179, 180, 181, 182, 183*
   boy with painted head, 176, *201*
   "Charlie Chaplin," 174, *199*
   English bisque, 175–176, *201*
   Maison Huret *bébé*, 172, *197*
   mechanical Théroude, 173, *198*
   Negro, 173–174, *177*
   "Rose Pierrette," 174–175, *200*
   waxed–papier-mâché, 172, *197*
Rawhide dolls, 54, 149
"Reading the News" (stereopticon card), *62*
Regency revival period, 172
Robbins, Kit, 57, 101, 129, 143
Robertson, Mrs. Norman, 31, 32
Rockingham porcelain figure, *86*
Rohmer, Marie, 112–113
Romantic period, 15, 21
Romantic Revival, 16, 45–48
"Rose Pierrette" (doll), 174–175, *200*
"Rough and the Doll" (illustration), *75*
Royal Berlin Porcelain Factory, 45
Royal Factory of Copenhagen, 46
Rubber dolls, 54, 55, *65, 92*, 149–150, *162*
Ruggles, Rowena Godding, 151
Ruskin, John, 90, 100

Schmitt et Fils (doll-makers), 128
"Schnickel-Fritz" (doll), 151
Schoenhut, Albert, 150, 151, 163, 164, 195
Sessions of the Peace, 3
Simon and Halbig (doll-makers), 129, 140, 144, 145, 147
Stuart period, 101
Switzerland, doll manufacture in, 3

"Tea and Coffee" (illustration), *87*
Théroude, Alexandre, 173, 198
Thompson, Martha, 187, 190, 191, 192, 193, 202
Thorpe, Ellery, 186–187, *189*
Toytown stories (Beaman), 17
Trade card, *77*

Upton, Florence K., 17

Vichy (firm), 180
Victoria, Queen, 18, 45, 112, 193
Victorian period, 53–57
"Virgin Mary" (doll), 18, *39*

"W. C. Fields" (doll), *169*
Walker, Izannah, 31–34, 43, 44
    rag dolls, 34, *40*
    secondary-layering process, 32
Wax, aesthetic qualities of, 68
Wax dolls *10, 11,* 67–72, *75, 76,* 77, *79, 80,*
        186
    categories of, 68
    composition, 68–71, *73, 75,* 77, *81, 95, 96,*
        172, 178, *196*
    made by craftsmen, 5
    made commercially, 5–6, *36*
    poured-, 70–71, *78, 79, 80, 95, 96*
Waxed–papier-mâché dolls, *see* Composition
    dolls

"Wedding Presents" (Champney), *130*
Weiderseim, Grace, *see* Drayton, Grace
Whitton, Margaret, 14, 19, 46, 54, 56, 99,
        129, 142, 150, 151, 154, 172, 188
"Wilson Children, The," *74*
Wind in the Willows, The (Grahame), 153
Woman's Home Companion (magazine), 151
Wooden dolls, *8,* 54, 68, 150–151, 186, *195*
    made by journeymen, 3–4
    with molded plaster faces, *26*

"Young Mother, The" (engraving), *24*
Your Dolls and Mine (Johl), 31